How the Reformation Began

How the Reformation Began

The Quincentennial Perspective

ANNA MARIE JOHNSON
NICHOLAS HOPMAN
EDITORS

PICKWICK *Publications* · Eugene, Oregon

HOW THE REFORMATION BEGAN
The Quincentennial Perspective

Pickwick Publications
An Imprint of Wipf and Stock Publishers
199 W. 8th Ave., Suite 3
Eugene, OR 97401

www.wipfandstock.com

PAPERBACK ISBN: 978-1-6667-3384-6
HARDCOVER ISBN: 978-1-6667-2880-4
EBOOK ISBN: 978-1-6667-2881-1

Cataloguing-in-Publication data:

Names: Johnson, Anna Marie, 1973–, editor. | Hopman, Nicholas, 1978–,
editor.

Title: How the Reformation began : the quincentennial perspective / edited by
Anna Marie Johnson and Nicholas Hopman.

Description: Eugene, OR: Pickwick Publications, 2022. | Includes bibliographi-
cal references.

Identifiers: ISBN 978-1-6667-3384-6 (paperback). | ISBN 978-1-6667-2880-4
(hardcover). | ISBN 978-1-6667-2881-1 (ebook).

Subjects: LCSH: Reformation. | Theology, Doctrinal—History—16th century. |
Luther, Martin, 1483–1546. | Church history—16th century.

Classification: BR305.3 H33 2022 (print). | BR305.3 (ebook).

03/21/22

Contents

Preface

ANNA MARIE JOHNSON

In 2017, the Reformation had a moment. With the 500th anniversary of the Ninety-five Theses, the Reformation was the subject of news stories, conferences, church services, and other commemorations. It was an unusual occurrence for a centuries-old religious movement that does not usually make the news, and Reformation specialists enjoyed the sudden relevance of their field. And then it was over. 2017 became 2018, and other historical milestones came into view.

Less casual observers of the Reformation know that the outcome of the indulgence controversy was anything but clear by 1518, or even by 1520. It could have been like so many other reform movements, that is, extinguished or rendered inconsequential with Luther's exile or execution. The years immediately after 1517 were particularly eventful, and those events helped shape the nascent movement. As word of Luther's challenge to indulgences spread, church officials debated how to respond to "the Luther affair," and both clergy and laity formed their own opinions. Meanwhile, discussions between Luther and church representatives took new turns, the issues for debate grew, and Luther's conviction deepened.

This collection of primary sources and commentary traces the route from Luther's critique of indulgences in the Ninety-five Theses to his condemnation at Worms in 1521. In between we see Luther articulating a theology of the cross, formulating his understanding of the sacraments, debating the limits of papal power, and outlining his ideals of Christian faith and life. We also see his opponents expressing their concerns, especially through the papal bulls, which explain the grounds for Luther's excommunication, and the emperor's edict declaring him an outlaw. Although the Diet of Worms in 1521 roundly condemned Luther and his ideas, the protection of his prince,

Frederick of Saxony, ensured the movement's survival. Frederick saved Luther from a martyr's fate by hiding him in the Wartburg Castle and, once Luther had returned to Wittenberg, by refusing to turn him over to authorities. Frederick's protection allowed Luther's burgeoning movement to build on the momentum it had gained and to establish new church structures despite clear repudiations by both the Roman Church and the imperial government in 1520 and 1521. Those new structures and the ideas they promoted would slowly change the face of the Western church and society.

This series of essays appeared in *Lutheran Quarterly* from 2017–2020 in advance of the 500th anniversary of each event. Each chapter introduces a foundational text or event, quotes key passages with commentary, and many suggest further reading. It was designed to help teachers and pastors respond to public interest in the anniversary of the Ninety-five Theses and to mine early Reformation themes for understanding and insight. All essays are reprinted here as they originally appeared in *Lutheran Quarterly*. See the concluding list of original publication credits.

I want to thank the authors who contributed their scholarly expertise to this series with accessible introductions and insightful commentaries, and those who helped prepare this book. Paul Rorem, *Lutheran Quarterly's* editor, conceived this book and organized its preparation. Martin Lohrmann and Nicholas Hopman assembled the documents with Hopman preparing the documents for publication. Managing Editor Virgil Thompson proposed this book to Wipf and Stock.

Abbreviations

AL   *The Annotated Luther*. 6 vols. Edited by Hans Hillerbrand et al. Minneapolis: Fortress, 2015

BC   *The Book of Concord*. Edited by Robert Kolb and Timothy J. Wengert. Minneapolis: Fortress, 2000

LW   *Luther's Works*. American Edition. 79 vols. Edited by Jaroslav Pelikan, Helmut Lehmann, and Christopher Boyd Brown. St. Louis and Philadelphia: Concordia and Fortress, 1955ff.

SLE   Johann Georg Walch, ed. *Dr. Martin Luthers Sämmtliche Schriften*. 25 vols. St. Louis: Lutherischer Concordia-Verlag, 1880–1910

WA   *Luthers Werke. Kritische Gesamtausgabe*. 57 vols. Edited by J. F. K. Knaake et al. Weimar: Böhlau, 1883ff.

WA Br   *Luthers Werke. Kritische Gesamtausgabe. Briefwechsel*. 11 vols. Weimar: Böhlau, 1930ff.

Contributors

THEODOR DIETER, Research Professor at the Institute for Ecumenical Research, Strasbourg, France.

KURT K. HENDEL, Professor Emeritus of Reformation History at the Lutheran School of Theology at Chicago.

SUZANNE HEQUET, Professor Emerita of Church History at Concordia University, St. Paul.

ERIK HERRMANN, Professor of Historical Theology at Concordia Seminary, St. Louis.

NICHOLAS HOPMAN, PhD Candidate in Church History at Princeton Theological Seminary, Princeton, New Jersey.

ANNA MARIE JOHNSON, Associate Professor of Reformation Church History at Garrett-Evangelical Theological Seminary, Evanston, Illinois.

RICHARD J. SERINA, PhD in Historical Theology, Associate Executive Director of the Commission on Theology and Church Relations, Lutheran Church—Missouri Synod, St. Louis.

MARK D. TRANVIK, Professor Emeritus of Religion at Augsburg University, Minneapolis.

TIMOTHY J. WENGERT, Professor Emeritus of Church History at United Lutheran Seminary, Philadelphia.

1

The 95 Theses (1517)

TIMOTHY J. WENGERT

THE YEAR 2017 IS the year to talk about the 95 *Theses* or, rather, talk around them, despite this author's translation and commentary. The usual suspects for such wandering around Luther's brief sentences are convinced that they have found either the first movement toward individual freedom by consciences bound in the twilight of the dark ages, or the clarion, religious call to reject all things Roman, or an invitation to be nice to our neighbors, whatever they may believe (the fallback position of American civil religion). Instead, lectures on the *Theses* should try to convince people to put them in their proper historical context rather than using them as an excuse to worship ourselves and our enlightened times.

The history of the 95 *Theses* and their medieval context may be found in other sources.[1] This essay concentrates instead on something of a conundrum, namely, why does Luther quote so little from the Bible? For someone, whom later generations wedded to the slogan *sola Scriptura*, this may seem rather odd. To be sure, these are theses, which Luther was then to prove using scripture passages, so that, indeed, there are many more references to scripture in Luther's defense, the so-called *Explanations of the 95 Theses*,

---

1. Timothy J. Wengert, *Martin Luther's 95 Theses* (Minneapolis: Fortress Press, 2015), xiii–xlvi; Berndt Hamm, *Ablass und Reformation: Erstaunliche Kohärenzen* (Tübingen: Mohr/Siebeck, 2016).

printed in August 1518.[2] But such a facile explanation does little to solve the riddle. The few important places where Luther directly deals with scripture come at the beginning and end of the document—a clue that will help us unravel how Luther is using scripture here.

PRELIMINARY REMARKS

Before going any further, however, readers need to be disabused of the centrality of *sola Scriptura* as a slogan describing Wittenberg's theology then or now. Philip Melanchthon never used the term, and Luther employed it in his Latin writings only twenty times (as opposed to 1200 for *sola fide* and 120 for *sola gratia* and 500 times for *solus Christus*).[3] Now, to be sure, he does use the phrase *solo Verbo* [by God's Word alone] on occasion, but there it is often hard to know whether Luther is talking about the preached word, the written Word, or both. In any case, as Scott Hendrix proved in his book on Luther and the papacy, Luther never abandoned other authorities besides scripture, so that the church fathers, the decrees of the councils and, above all, the catholic creeds also were authoritative for him throughout his life—as they should be for later Lutherans.[4] Peter Fraenkel, the Melanchthon scholar, writing in the 1960s, found a far better Latin phrase in Melanchthon's writings—one that could more accurately replace *sola Scriptura* in stained-glass windows.[5] For Luther and his colleagues, scripture was the *primum et verum*, the first and true authority, the other authorities being always derivative, resting upon their ability to witness, like John the Baptist, to the Lamb of God who takes away the sin of the world.

Of course, there are certain allusions to scripture scattered throughout the *Theses*. In Thesis 11, the bishops were sleeping when some evil person sowed such bad theology regarding papal power to grant indulgences (Matt. 13:25). Thesis 26 refers to papal authority as the power of the keys, echoing Matthew 16:19. Giving to the poor and lending to the needy, mentioned in Thesis 43, reflect Matthew 5:42. Fishing for the wealthy with the nets of the gospel and making the first last, while clearly scriptural (Matt. 13:47; 19:30), are simply employed to underscore the evil motives of indulgence

---

2. Martin Luther, *Explanations of the 95 Theses* (1518) in LW 31:77–252.

3. Timothy J. Wengert, "A Note on 'Sola Scriptura' in Martin Luther's Writings," *Luther-Bulletin* 20 (2011): 21–31; Wengert, *Reading the Bible with Martin Luther* (Grand Rapids: Baker, 2013), 16–21.

4. Scott Hendrix, *Luther and the Papacy: Stages in a Reformation Conflict* (Philadelphia: Fortress, 1981).

5. Peter Fraenkel, *Testimonia Patrum: The Function of the Patristic Argument in the Theology of Philip Melanchthon* (Geneva: Droz, 1961).

preachers. Even so, outside of the very first and last theses, these are nearly all the clear allusions to scripture.

Luther's reticence at this point cannot be chalked up to his lack of experience with the scripture. Instead, his limited use of scripture in this setting demonstrates his respect for reading the biblical text in context. Moreover, as he will later plead against Karlstadt and other "ravers" as he nicknamed them, when one reads something in scripture, one cannot simply ask, "Is it the Word of God?" but rather, "Is it the Word of God for us?"[6]

Luther's example also clears the way for Lutheran Christians to use their heads. His fierce logic and remarkable rhetoric in the 95 Theses remind us of that saying in Proverbs 25:11: "A word fitly spoken is like apples of gold in settings of silver." In short, the 95 Theses is death to all manner of specious proof texting. Indeed, when Luther or Melanchthon refer to a single verse of scripture, one must first search out and understand their interpretation of the text in its exegetical context before dismissing their arguments.[7]

THE RHETORIC OF THE 95 THESES

So, Luther puts his most important scriptural arguments at the beginning and end of the Theses. Why? Here a recent insight in the study of the 95 Theses may help.[8] Luther's work has a rhetorical shape. This is not to say that Luther did not also use logic or dialectics, as he called it. But the overall shape of the Theses is imbued with important aspects of Renaissance rhetoric—much as in Freedom of Christian, as Birgit Stolt demonstrated in the 1960s, or as in the Invocavit Sermons of 1522, as Neil Leroux has proved more recently.[9] This means that we can identify the typical parts of a Renaissance speech here, an argument strengthened by the fact that in his Explanations Luther labels two sections with technical names and writes his defense as if his arguments were meant to be read in this rhetorical light.

6. Martin Luther, How Christians Should Regard Moses (1525) in LW 35:170. See Vitor Westhelle, The Church Event: Call and Challenge of a Church Protestant (Minneapolis: Fortress, 2010), 65–68.

7. This is one of the weaknesses of the "New Perspectives on Paul" and their criticisms of the reformers.

8. The author first stumbled upon this insight while collaborating with an ecumenical group of European scholars working on a new German translation and commentary of the Theses.

9. Birgit Stolt, Studien zu Luthers Freiheitstraktat mit besonderer Rücksicht auf das Verhältnis der lateinischen und der deutschen Fassung zu einander und die Stilmittel der Rhetorik (Stockholm: Almzvist & Wiksell, 1969); Neil R. Leroux, Luther's Rhetoric: Strategies and Style from the Invocavit Sermons (St. Louis: Concordia, 2002).

These parts are traditionally, in this order, the exordium (introduction), the narration (basic, commonly accepted facts), the main thesis (summarized in Thesis 5), the proof or confirmation of this thesis and its corollaries, the refutation of anticipated objections, and the peroration.[10] In the exordium, on which Luther puts great weight in his prefatory letter for the *Explanations* addressed to Pope Leo X, Luther writes that he is presenting these theses "out of love and zeal for the truth."[11] The proof of his work stretches from theses 1–80, and a rejection or confutation of other opinions—placed in the mouth of a sharp layperson—comes in theses 81–91. Crucial for Luther's interpretation of scripture, however, comes in the narration and the peroration: theses 1–4 and 91–95. Precisely where Luther sets forth the incontrovertible facts at the beginning and a summary of his argument at the end, he calls upon scripture.

THE NARRATION: MATTHEW 4:17

In traditional rhetoric, the narration is an exposition of the facts of the case, on which both the main thesis and its confirmation rest. The narration, as Cicero or Quintilian explain it, involves presenting facts that are presumably not in dispute, but rather accepted by all. Sure enough, in his *Explanations* Luther declares that these first four theses are *not* up for debate. Moreover, his educated readers would most likely have agreed with him, because Luther's entire case rests upon a single verse of scripture and the "newest" accepted facts about it. His fellow humanists surely knew it—especially once Luther unpacked it in the *Explanations* published in August 1518. The first thesis is thus the bedrock upon which Luther's entire argument rests. "Our Lord and Master Jesus Christ, in saying 'Do penance . . . ,' wanted the entire life of the faithful to be one of penitence."[12]

Luther is quoting the standard Vulgate rendering of Matthew 4:17 (*Poenitentiam agite*). The older English version of the *Theses*, strongly influenced by the very arguments under investigation here, translates it "Repent."[13] In Latin and German, however, the same phrase may be rendered "Do penance," "Be penitent," or "Repent." Luther's contemporaries would thus have heard in Jesus' words a command to avail themselves of the sacrament of

---

10. For the fuller argument, see *Luther's 95 Theses*, 5–8 and Timothy J. Wengert, "The Ninety-Five Theses as a Literary and Theological Event," *Luther-Jahrbuch* 85 (2018): 37–60 (an address to the 2017 International Luther Congress meeting in Wittenberg).

11. WA 1:528.

12. *Luther's 95 Theses*, 13.

13. LW 31:25.

penance. But Luther knew better, not because *he* had discovered a new approach to this text (a singular addiction of the modern age to novelty but worrisome to Luther) but rather because the year before, in 1516, the famous Greek scholar, Erasmus of Rotterdam, had published for the first time the Greek New Testament, printed in parallel columns with the Latin Vulgate. We know from Luther's lectures on Romans that he immediately got hold of a copy and was teaching himself Greek while, at the same time, using the companion volume of Erasmus' annotations that explained where the Vulgate needed correction on the basis of the Greek text.

Sure enough, in comments on Matthew 4:17 Erasmus referred his readers back to comments on Matthew 3:2, where John the Baptist uses the same phrase. At that place, Erasmus pointed out that the Greek, *metanoiete*, is better translated as "change your hearts" or "change your minds." But he did more. He pointed out that with Jerome's Latin translation the church fathers, Augustine in particular, connected this text to the public punishment of flagrant sinners. Only in the Middle Ages did some theologians commit the "not small error," as Erasmus puts it, of then applying Augustine's statements on this text to the medieval sacrament of penance.

Now, although Luther could have judged Erasmus' insight as "new," he did not, because both he and Erasmus, as humanists, were committed to the cry, *ad fontes*, back to the sources, where the oldest sources were always deemed the purest and best. Thus, before correcting the original Latin translation of Jerome, Erasmus carefully disentangles Jesus' words from questionable medieval usage, based upon a misunderstanding of a church father. In the *Explanations* Luther, without naming Erasmus, makes his dependence on the Dutch humanist clear by citing the Greek text and explaining to the reader what it means.

Already this indicates a crucial aspect of proper biblical interpretation in the church for Luther. It never occurs in a vacuum but is part of the continuing conversation on the sacred text's meaning stretching from within the Bible itself to the present. The notion of the lone reader of scripture, sitting in a motel room armed only with his or her King James Version of the Bible and coming to faith, destroys the church and is built upon a myth of individualism that continues to distort modern and postmodern interpretation of scripture in America.[14] On the contrary, Luther and other Wit-

---

14. I still remember my first semester at Luther Seminary, when each week professors had to meet with their junior advisees. So I dutifully sat in Roy Harrisville's office with two or three others, one of whom, a dyed-in-the-wool fundamentalist, challenged Harrisville on every biblical point imaginable. Finally, out of desperation, the student demanded to know what could possibly prevent the good professor from letting the text mean whatever he wanted it to. Harrisville, never known for understating an argument,

tenberg reformers did not read the Bible alone but always in conversation with contemporaries and, even more importantly, with their predecessors.[15]

But on this particular text, Luther does Erasmus one better, bringing insights gleaned from his recent lectures on Romans into his understanding of the Matthean text. Indeed, a single word turns the world this text addresses upside down: "the *entire* life." This is such a profound insight into the biblical text, but one that few people appreciate. With a single sentence, based upon a particular reading of Matthew, Luther has destroyed the single most pernicious view of the Christian life lurking among Christians today: that there is a before and after in the Christian life. "Once I was a sinner; now I am a believer." "Once I was in a state of sin; now I am in a state of grace."

This division of the Christian life into a before and after means that certain biblical texts, such as Matthew 4:17, only apply at certain times in a Christian's life—whether applied to penance and penitence from the Vulgate or even to a change of mind and repentance implied by *metanoiete*. But Luther realized that such a view sells the biblical text and its speaker, Jesus Christ, short. As long as human beings think that they have graduated from repentance to living a Christian life or doing really good, meritorious works, the Bible seems to become remarkably silent—precisely at the point where it most applies to us. "Repent!" Jesus says, and we look around the room and think, "Too bad so-and-so isn't here, because he or she really needs to hear this!" Or, "It's *those* people who need to repent!" Or, worse yet, we think, "But I've tried to no avail! The good that I would that I do not; the evil that I would not, that I do!" Then, instead of invoking the savior—"Thanks be to God through Jesus Christ our Lord!"—we simply despair, assuming there must be something we have failed to do or left undone.

Luther had already expressed this notion the year before in his lectures on Romans 7—helped by Augustine, where neither exegete possessed the West's "introspective conscience."[16] So, in the first, unassailable thesis of the 95 *Theses* Luther insists that Christian believers are, to use the phrase that already occurs in comments on Romans 7, *simul iustus et peccator* (simultaneously a righteous person and a sinner). This is meant not in the gross antinomian way that some today use it ("Ha! We all make mistakes!"), but rather precisely as a description of one's entire life: captive to sin, unable to free oneself. By breaking the connection to penance, Erasmus had undercut

---

waved his arms around his office, pointing to the hundreds of tomes that surrounded us and said, "The church, Norm, the church!"

15. See Robert Kolb, *Martin Luther and the Enduring Word of God: The Wittenberg School and Its Scripture-Centered Proclamation* (Grand Rapids: Baker, 2016).

16. See the unfortunate essay by Krister Stendal, "The Apostle Paul and the Introspective Conscience of the West," *Harvard Theological Review* 56 (1963): 199–215.

this text's ritual use; by referring to the Christian's "entire life," Luther re-stated the truly good news about God's remedy for human sin, removing all limitations to the application of Jesus' words for the hearer.

In this way the *Theses* constitute a debate over the law's function in the life of the Christian. This gets to the very heart of Luther's questioning of late-medieval practices of indulgences. Already in a sermon delivered at the Castle Church on 16 January 1517, as part of the celebration of the anniversary of that church's dedication in 1503, to which an indulgence of 200 days was attached, Luther expressed his deep concerns regarding indulgences.[17] How could indulgences, he asked, correspond to the Christian life of faith that welcomed God's discipline and chastisement of the flesh. This sermon disconcerted poor elector Frederick, who rather loved his religious foundations and saw himself as the head of religious life in Saxony. In response to the prince's objections and to rumors about the exaggerated preaching of Johann Tetzel that had just started in January in Luther's birthplace, Eisleben, Luther began to do his theological homework, discovering in the process that indulgences had a completely different, wholly pastoral and ecclesial function in the early church and, more importantly, discovering that Jesus' command to "Do penance" had nothing to do with the medieval sacrament. From his study of Paul, Luther already knew that God was constantly in hot pursuit of humanity, working death to the old creature and life to the new. He summarized this central insight with the simple phrase, "the entire life." This means that one cannot somehow opt out of the law's condemnation by any religious action whatsoever. The entire life of a Christian consists in death and resurrection.

Yet if we reduce this to a theological concept, Luther's hermeneutical revolution passes us by and we are bound to reintroduce some form of the "before and after" shape of Christianity into our interpretation of scripture. Melanchthon's famous dictum, *lex semper accusat* (the law always accuses), is not a paean to the law's eternality but to humanity's incapacity to escape the law by its own powers. But even this does not reach the heart of Luther's surprising exegetical insight. By applying this dictum of Jesus to the entire life of a Christian, Christ suddenly speaks directly and unequivocally to the hearer. The electing voice of God sounds out: "Change your minds!" Once

17. See Timothy J. Wengert, "Martin Luther's Preaching an Indulgence in January 1517," *Lutheran Quarterly* 29 (2015): 62–75. The notion, proposed by Franz Posset, *The Front-Runner of the Catholic Reformation: The Life and Works of Johann von Staupitz* (Aldershot, UK: Ashgate, 2003), that Johann von Staupitz put Luther up to attacking indulgences completely misreads the situation in 1517. Luther's work, stimulated by his own trouble preaching an indulgence and Tetzel's exaggerated claims, used Erasmus, canon law, Johann Eck, Johann von Paltz, along with von Staupitz's 1516 sermons as sources.

no exegetical sleight-of-hand can avoid this demand, the hearers are caught precisely in their inability to do what Christ demands, to repent. Then God must speak another word that simultaneously frees from guilt and punishment—to say nothing of doubt, fear, death, law, conscience, and evil. Yet that freeing word does not cause the hearers to avoid the death of the law but forces them *through* death to life—daily—until death finally puts an end to the struggle.

Then, too, Luther's later question to Karlstadt, "Does this word apply to me?" takes on new sharpness. Unlike the list of moral do's and don't's that threaten to drown Karlstadt and his Puritan descendants, where one can surely ask, "Does the Jubilee, the keeping of Sabbath, or the tithe apply to me?" Luther insists that Jesus speaks directly and unconditionally, demanding not simply obedience to a set of external rules by which we can measure our goodness but instead demanding the entire life of the Christian. The very prima facie impossibility of Jesus' command ("Change your mind!") defines its universal applicability to us. Of course, the old creature still wants to slither out from under it—but always with some form of before and after. Once Christ addresses the "entire life" of a Christian, all such shadowboxing is over and the Word of Christ does its worst to us. Only then is this word a *viva vox*, a living word, "sharper than any two-edged sword, dividing soul and spirit, joint and marrow" (Heb. 4:12). Then the law truly is, as my teacher Gerhard Forde used to say, the cutting edge of the gospel.

This early language of Luther, then, relates to two central aspects of his theology: justification by faith alone and baptism. Regarding justification, Oswald Bayer demonstrated in his doctoral work, *Promissio*, that Luther at this stage in his career was still struggling to define faith.[18] Having inherited Augustine's understanding of humility as the best definition of faith, Luther still imagined that although positive works did not contribute to a person's relation to God, the Christian still had to demonstrate complete humility—giving God all the glory and giving up all claims to righteousness. But this still left the door open to a form of works righteousness by negation—like the pastor who is humble but then proud that he was humble, and then humble that he was proud that he was humble, and so on. As Luther worked on his *Explanations* of the 95 *Theses*, Bayer argues, he came to realize that this very faith and trust in God is not in human control at all but rather a work that God carries out through God's Word. Thus, he explained Thesis 62 ("The true treasure of the church is the most holy gospel of the glory and grace of God") in this way.

18. Oswald Bayer, *Promissio: Geschichte der reformatorischen Wende in Luthers Theologie* (Göttingen: Vandenhoeck & Ruprecht, 1971).

> [The gospel] is a word of salvation, a word of grace, a word of comfort, a word of joy, a voice of the bridegroom and the bride, a good word, a word of peace . . . But the law is a word of destruction, a word of wrath, a word of sadness, a word of grief, a voice of the judge and the defendant, a word of restlessness, a word of curse . . . Through the law we have nothing except an evil conscience, a restless heart, a troubled breast because of our sins, which the law points out but does not take away. And we ourselves cannot take it away. Therefore for those of us who are held captive . . . the light of the gospel comes and says: "Fear not," "comfort, comfort my people," . . . "behold the Lamb of God who takes away the sin of the world." Behold that one who alone fulfils the law for you . . . When the sinful conscience hears this sweetest messenger it comes to life again, shouts for joy while leaping about full of confidence . . .[19]

Of this certainty we hear only faint echoes in the *Theses* themselves, where Luther will insist on trusting the complete remission of guilt through the word of the priest in thesis six and defines the true treasure of the church as the "Gospel of the grace and glory of God." Throughout his early lectures, we also find foreshadowed this insight into the Word that works on us, which he finally states clearly in the *Explanations*.[20] Indeed, Luther's destruction of "before-and-after Christianity" only arises when Christ's word addresses us directly. Thus, Bayer helps us to see the clearest early expression of Luther's insight: that the direct address itself *does* what it says, giving through faith alone the very change of mind the law demands.

Without saying one word about baptism in the *Theses*, Luther nevertheless also foreshadowed here his later conviction that baptism is the heart and soul of the Christian life. Thus, in the Large Catechism, we hear the culmination of Luther's argument, expressed already in 1520 in the *Babylonian Captivity of the Church*, that being baptized constitutes the entire life of the believer and that the sacrament of absolution, as the Wittenbergers renamed the sacrament of penance, was nothing more or less than a return to baptism.

> These two parts, being dipped under the water and emerging from it, point to the power and effect of Baptism, which is nothing else than the slaying of the old Adam and the resurrection of the new creature, both of which must continue in us our whole

19. LW 31:231.

20. For a far more nuanced view of the development of Luther's theology, see Berndt Hamm, *The Early Luther: Stages in a Reformation Reorientation*, trans. Martin Lohrmann (Grand Rapids: Eerdmans, 2014).

life long. Thus a Christian life is nothing else than a daily Baptism, begun once and continuing ever after. For we must keep at it without ceasing, always purging whatever pertains to the old Adam, so that whatever belongs to the new creature may come forth.[21]

THE PERORATION: JEREMIAH 6:14

Thesis 92: "And thus, away with all those prophets who say to Christ's people, 'Peace, peace,' and there is no peace!" The pre-critical immediacy with which Luther applies a prophetic word to his own situation may at first cause some pause among those wedded to certain forms of non-contextualized biblical interpretation. But Luther's dilemma is an urgent one: how can a theologian depict accurately the result of bad preaching in the church? From Thesis 21, where he first takes aim at the indulgence preachers, through to the end of the *Theses* his worry is the misleading things coming out of preachers' mouths. Luther realizes that his duty cannot simply be a bourgeois blessing of the status quo. Pious encouragement to "do what is in you," and promises that "God helps those who help themselves" have devolved in this age into a prosperity gospel that even Johann Tetzel himself would have been ashamed to proclaim. Yet few have the courage to admonish wayward colleagues who have exchanged God's blessing for a mess of moralistic pottage.

But there is far more going on in Luther's citation of Jeremiah than his inability or unwillingness to draw distinctions between his own age and Jeremiah's or, in other circumstances, Paul's. This only becomes clear in the next thesis, which cleverly interprets the text of Jeremiah in the light of Christ. "May it go well for all of those prophets who say to Christ's people, 'Cross, cross,' and there is no cross!" Insofar as this peroration contains a summary of Luther's arguments, these two theses could be said to summarize the main point of the narration that we have already outlined above. The Christian life goes *through* the cross to peace not around the cross, as the sale of letters of indulgence implied. Insofar as the sale of indulgences claimed to lift the burden of God's chastising discipline, it was no different from Jeremiah's false prophets, who promised peace and thus avoided the cross.

Slightly more than a year before the *Theses* were written, Luther had penned a letter of encouragement to an Augustinian prior, Michael Dressel,

---

21. Martin Luther, *The Large Catechism*, Baptism, par. 65, in BC 465.

who had just been removed from office by his disgruntled brothers.[22] In response to his complaining, Luther wrote these words:

> Are you ignorant, most honorable father, that God . . . places his peace in the midst of no peace, that is, in the midst of all trials? . . . Therefore, that person whom no one disturbs does not have peace—on the contrary, this is the peace of the world. Instead, that person whom everyone and everything disturbs has peace and bears all of these things with quiet joy. You are saying with Israel, "Peace, peace, and there is no peace"; instead say with Christ, "Cross, cross, and there is no cross." For as quickly as the cross ceases to be cross so quickly you would say joyfully [with the hymn], 'Blessed cross, among the trees there is none such [as you]."[23]

This remarkable epistolary gloss on Luther's cryptic comments in the 95 Theses allows us to place these final statements squarely within Luther's theology of the cross, thus giving us a second vantage point from which to understand Luther's approach to scripture.[24] The old creature, hardwired to be self-centered, cannot see any good in suffering and will go to any lengths to avoid it. Thus, for the sinner the cross of Christ—to say nothing of the suffering of human beings—is a conundrum, only able to be explained with complicated theories that place the meaning of the crucifixion either on God's shoulders (as in Anselm) or our shoulders (as in Abelard) or on the devil's shoulders (as in the ancient church).[25] But such theories of the atonement and others like them often only provide ways to avoid the cross and its horrible judgment on all humanity.

Luther, on the contrary, urges Dressel to go through the cross, not around it. Our urge to make theological peace with God, whether liberal or conservative, provides only a hollow victory, what Luther in the *Explanations*

22. For this connection, I am indebted to Augustinus Sander, who first pointed me to this very important source for Theses 92–93.

23. 23 June 1516 in WA Br 1:27, 38–46. Luther is quoting verse six of "Pange lingua" ("Sing, My Tongue").

24. Luther was by no means the only late-medieval theologian to express what later historians have labeled the theology of the cross. Johannes Tauler and other so-called German mystics also noted the paradoxical ways of God's approach to human beings and their reason. See Timothy J. Wengert, "'Peace, Peace . . . Cross, Cross': Reflections on How Martin Luther Relates the Theology of the Cross to Suffering," *Theology Today* 59 (2002): 190–205; Gerhard O. Forde, *On Being a Theologian of the Cross: Reflections on Luther's Heidelberg Disputation, 1518* (Grand Rapids: Eerdmans, 1997).

25. See Gustaf Aulén, *Christus Victor: An Historical Study of the Three Main Types of the Idea of the Atonement*, trans. A. G. Hebert, foreword by Jaroslav Pelikan (New York: Macmillan, 1969).

of the 95 Theses calls a *theologia illusoria* (a make-believe theology).[26] The theology of the cross insists on telling the truth about humanity and God, calling a thing what it is. It reveals humanity's deepest denials and, at the same time, witnesses to God's revelation *sub contrario specie*, under the appearance of the opposite: God in the last place we would reasonably look.

This juxtaposition of the human addiction to peace next to God's activity under the cross puts the lie to every human-centered reading of the Bible. Whether we use the Bible to wring out of it a cherished doctrine, a moral principle or imperative, or a star chart for the future, we cry with Israel, "Peace, peace," and join the hosts of false prophets, addicted to right doctrine, right morals and right predictions, simply echoing the three imagined "spiritual" meanings of scripture from the Middle Ages: *allegoria*, *tropologia* and *anagogia*. Despite Luther's complete dismissal of indulgence preachers—ancient and modern—our own age's prophets, like his, continue with abandon this assault on God's Word.

When applied to scripture, the theology of the cross does not mean that whatever the text says, we are to make it mean the opposite. Instead it means that whatever the text says about God and humanity is already the opposite of our reasonable—that is, self-centered—approaches to scripture. The problem with all human approaches to the Bible is the same: we recast it in our own image, make it obey our most cherished hopes and dreams by avoiding the cross and championing peace and piety, judgment and justice, theology and theodicy. Moreover, our approaches to scripture also assume that, at some level, scripture is strong and not subject to the vagaries of our human existence. But the cross reveals the strength of a divinely weak word, a crucified God, and a justified sinner.

At the same time, this hermeneutic of the cross, if one may call it that, insists on a preacher in the present bestowing in his or her own weakness the cross upon the hearer. True, Isaiah said, "Thus says the Lord." But if all the preacher does is describe in glowing terms Isaiah's own inspiration ("He really nailed it for good old Hezekiah!"), then the scripture falls strangely silent. On the contrary, the preacher must fulfill the office of prophet in his or her own words. Just as we do not say: "I hope this is the body of Christ for you, but who knows?" or "I guess I'm baptizing you in the name of the Triune God," the pastor or preacher dare not say, in the absolution, "May God forgive you," or "God forgive you," as if we weren't sure, but rather, "As a called and ordained minister of the church of Christ and by his authority, I announce to you the entire forgiveness of all your sins—no ifs, ands, or buts

---

26. LW 31:225.

about it. Were it up to me, given our last council meeting, I wouldn't forgive any of you. But it's not; it's up to Christ crucified."

The same is true from the pulpit. Here Luther's obsession with bad preaching in the 95 *Theses* comes to full expression in *Freedom of a Christian*, which can best be read as a handbook for gospel-centered preaching.[27] Smack dab in the middle of this 1520 treatise, Luther provides for his readers both trenchant criticism of his age's own preachers and a brief outline of true, evangelical preaching. First comes the criticism.

> I believe that it has become clear that it is not sufficient or even Christian if, as those who are the very best preachers today do, we only preach Christ's works, life and words just as a kind of story or as historical exploits (which would be enough to know in providing an example of how to conduct our lives). Much worse is when there is complete silence about Christ, and human laws and the decrees of the fathers are taught instead of Christ. Moreover, some even preach Christ and recite stories about him for this purpose: to play on human emotions either to arouse sympathy for him or to incite anger against the Jews. This kind of thing is simply childish and over-emotional nonsense.[28]

Note what Luther is implying. Preaching the narrative—particularly popular in our day—gets you no further than treating Christ like a really good example: that really sainted elder brother to which your mother was always comparing you. So what if people know the difference between Abraham and Jacob or can recite the history of salvation from beginning to end! It finally only provides fine moral examples for us to follow—well, excepting that crook Jacob, of course. But others get wrapped up in human laws: the law of paying off a debt to Thrivent; of attracting more members to the congregation so that the pastor feels good about himself or herself; of toeing the politically correct line—left or right: as if social action or passing legislation or getting favorable Supreme Court justices ever made a difference in our standing before God. Worse yet, there are those who simply pluck at our emotional heartstrings, so that we may get angry at unbelievers or get sorry that Christ suffered or get happy that Judas landed in hell. We do not find salvation by getting the facts straight, by following the rules or by feeling bad!

> So Luther must rewrite the preaching manuals—in his day and ours alike.

27. See Timothy J. Wengert, "Luther's *Freedom of a Christian* for Today's Church," *Lutheran Quarterly* 28 (2014): 1–21.

28. Martin Luther, *Freedom of a Christian* (1520/21), in AL 1:508.

> Preaching, however, ought to serve this goal: that faith in Christ
> is promoted. Then he is not simply "Christ" but "Christ for you
> and me," and what we say about him and call him affect us. This
> faith is born and preserved by preaching why Christ came, what
> he brought and gave, and what are the needs and the fruit that
> his reception entail. This kind of preaching occurs where Chris-
> tian freedom is rightly taught, freedom that we gain from him
> and that makes us Christians all kings and priests.[29]

Christ for you! This simple summary of good Lutheran preaching does
not merely change what comes out of our mouths, it transforms what we
read with our eyes. The point of the four gospels—and what makes them
so different from all the other "gospels" running around out there—is their
common conviction that they are writing about Christ "for us."[30] John
20:31–31 states it most plainly: "These things were written so that you might
believe . . ." No wonder that in the history of biblical interpretation it was
first a Wittenberg exegete and student of Luther and Philip Melanchthon,
namely, Caspar Cruciger Sr., who insisted that this verse formed the basic
argument of the entire book.[31]

But the other Gospel writers are also bent upon underscoring the "for
you," of Jesus' message, life, death and resurrection. When reading Matthew,
do not succumb to the siren calls of modern interpreters, who trumpet every command they find there. Instead, take heart in the fact that Matthew
is the gospel of Immanuel, God with us, a theme first struck in the very
first chapter and repeated in chapters 18 ("where two are three are gathered,
there I am") and 28 ("Lo! I am with you always").[32] And Matthew puts forgiveness where it belongs: precisely in the community's gathering around
bread and wine, the body and blood of Christ, "for the forgiveness of sins."
Mark, that preeminent theologian of the cross, destroys all our human efforts to capture and tame God, announcing in the very first verse that this is
"The Gospel of Jesus Christ, Son of God." It is not the rules of Jesus Christ,
another lawgiver. And almost every story in the book points to the miracle
of faith, until the last person you would ever think could do it, exclaims at
the foot of the cross, "Surely this is God's Son." And Luke? Already Philip
Melanchthon pointed to the centrality of the final chapter and its description of true penitence: We preach the crucified and risen Christ so that

29. AL 1:508.

30. See Wengert, *Reading the Bible*, 58–68.

31. Timothy J. Wengert, "Caspar Cruciger Sr.'s 1546 'Enarratio' on John's Gospel: An
Experiment in Ecclesiological Exegesis," *Church History* 61 (1992): 60–74.

32. Something I learned from my colleague, Prof. Robin Mattison.

"Repentance and forgiveness of sins may be preached to the entire world." Every time we wander off into Jesus' exploits, or center on his moral injunctions, or, in Luther's words elsewhere, try to make old women cry, then there is no "for you." Then the Bible means nothing at all.

FINAL REMARKS

Was anyone listening? Did Luther's approach to scripture as a foolish word that does death and resurrection to us our entire lives have any effect on the readers of his day or of ours? In the first instance, theologically speaking, we must say no, precisely because the Word that tells the truth about the human condition and God's mercy as law and gospel encounters hearts of stone. We cannot believe what reveals the very worst about us, and we cannot believe the electing mercy of God. No! The Word must finally do its deed to us, kill and make alive—daily—so that we may finally experience the freedom of the Word.

But, historically speaking, the answer must be yes. Consider Philip Melanchthon's take on *poenitentia* in the Augsburg Confession and its Apology. In the Confession he wrote: "Now properly speaking, true repentance is nothing else than to have contrition and sorrow, or terror about sin and yet *at the same time* to believe in the gospel and absolution that sin is forgiven and grace is obtained through Christ. Such faith, in turn, comforts the heart and puts it at peace."[33] The move from terror to comfort is precisely the *"simul iustus et peccator"* at the heart of Luther's law/gospel hermeneutic. Melanchthon makes the connection even clearer in the Apology. "Wherever Paul describes conversion or renewal, he almost always distinguishes these two parts, putting to death and making alive," Melanchthon notes. And then he continues:

> However, what need is there to cite so many testimonies when they are obvious throughout the Scriptures? Psalm 118[:18], "The Lord has punished me severely, but he did not give me over to death." Psalm 119[:28], "My soul melts away for sorrow; strengthen me according to your Word." Here the first part contains contrition, while the second clearly describes how we are revived in the midst of contrition, namely by the Word of God that offers grace. This Word sustains and gives life to the heart. 1 Samuel 2 [:6]: "The Lord kills and brings to life; he brings down to Sheol and raises up." In each of these, the first part refers to contrition; the second part refers to faith. Also Isaiah 28[:21],

33. Augsburg Confession XII.3–5, in BC 44.

"For the Lord will rise up as on Mount Perazim, he will rage as in the valley of Gibeon; to do his deed—strange is his deed! and to work his work—alien is his work!" He calls it an alien work of God to terrify, because the proper work of God is to make alive and console. But he terrifies, he says, in order to make room for consolation and vivification because hearts that do not feel the wrath of God loathe consolation in their smugness. In this way, Scripture makes a practice of joining these two things, terrors and consolation, in order to teach that these are the chief parts of repentance: contrition and faith that consoles and justifies . . . For these are the two chief works of God in human beings, to justify the terrified or make them alive. The entire Scripture is divided into these two works. One part is the law, which reveals, denounces, and condemns sin. The second part is the gospel, that is, the promise of grace given in Christ.[34]

This alien and proper work of God through the Word, bringing about death and resurrection, terror and comfort, precisely matches the scriptural basis of the 95 Theses. This uniquely Lutheran hermeneutic arises again and again in the early history of Lutheranism—where law and gospel are not attempts to divide commands and promises but to discern God's strange work of death and proper work of resurrection—putting to death the old and bringing to life the new in us and for us.

The best way to commemorate this 500th anniversary, therefore, is not to dress up in a black robe with a doctor's cap and pretend to be Martin Luther nor to hammer some fiery theses upon a church door somewhere, but rather to preach the gospel. It won't hurt. Perhaps after a year one could go back to reciting narratives and moralizing and manipulating listeners emotionally. But for this year, one need only look the people in the eye and say, "This Jesus is for you, no holds barred!" If that doesn't kill them and make them all alive, nothing can.

This essay is based upon the Hein-Fry/Book of Faith keynote lecture given in April 2017 at the Lutheran Theological Seminary at Philadelphia and at Luther Seminary in St. Paul, Minnesota.

---

34. Philip Melanchthon, *Apology of the Augsburg Confession* (September 1531), XII.49–53, in BC 195.

2

The Heidelberg Disputation (1518)

NICHOLAS HOPMAN

AMID THE TURMOIL SURROUNDING Martin Luther's 95 Theses, he was invited to introduce his theology at the tri-annual meeting of his Augustinian Hermits order in Heidelberg. The Heidelberg Disputation took place on April 26, 1518, in the lecture hall of the liberal arts faculty at the University. For this occasion Luther carefully crafted twenty-eight theological theses and proofs along with twelve philosophical theses attacking Aristotle. He impressed Johannes Brenz (Württemberg), Martin Bucer (Strasbourg), and several other significant future reformers who attended the disputation.

Luther here began to define several theological concepts that together would play an essential role throughout his career. His theological anthropology contradicted the scholastic dictum *facere quod in se est* (do what is within you, namely, do your best) by attacking free will itself (Thesis 13), and identifying human righteousness, even before the fall, as passive. He claimed that God's law cannot create righteousness but only sin (Thesis 23). Luther contrasted the law and its works with the gospel and faith in Christ (Theses 21–26). The Heidelberg Disputation is also the *locus classicus* for Luther's theology of the cross (Theses 11–21). He contrasted theologians of glory, who interpret God in terms of the good, the true, and the beautiful, with theologians of the cross, who comprehend God in his human nature, in weakness, foolishness, and suffering in Christ. In accordance with this distinction, Luther defined the creative love of God, which makes something out of nothing, in opposition to sinful human love, which is attracted by what is already good or beautiful (Thesis 28). The theology of the cross articulated in the Heidelberg Disputation also previewed Luther's teaching on the hidden God (*deus absconditus*), as God hides his eternal glory and instead reveals himself in death itself.

TEXT

13. *Free will, after the fall, exists in name only, and as long as it does what it is able to do, it commits a mortal sin.*

The first part is clear, for the will is captive and subject to sin. Not that it is nothing, but that it is not free except to do evil. According to John 8[:34, 36], "Every one who commits sin is a slave to sin . . . So if the Son makes you free, you will be free indeed." Hence St. Augustine says in his book, *The Spirit and the Letter*, "Free will without grace has the power to do nothing but sin"; and in the second book of *Against Julian*, "You call the will free, but in fact it is an enslaved will," and in many other places.

The second part is clear from what has been said above and from the verse in Hos. 13[:9], "Israel, you are bringing misfortune upon yourself, for your salvation is alone with me," and from similar passages.[1]

19. *That person does not deserve to be called a theologian who looks upon the invisible things of God as though they were clearly perceptible in those things which have actually happened [Rom. 1:20].*

This is apparent in the example of those who were "theologians" and still were called fools by the Apostle in Rom. 1[:22]. Furthermore, the invisible things of God are virtue, godliness, wisdom, justice, goodness, and so forth. The recognition of all these things does not make one worthy or wise.

20. *He deserves to be called a theologian, however, who comprehends the visible and manifest things of God seen through suffering and the cross.*

The "back" and visible things of God are placed in opposition to the invisible, namely, his human nature, weakness, foolishness. The Apostle in I Cor. 1[:25] calls them the weakness and folly of God. Because men misused the knowledge of God through works, God wished again to be recognized in suffering, and to condemn wisdom concerning invisible things by means of wisdom concerning visible things, so that those who did not honor God as manifested in his works should honor him as he is hidden in his suffering. As the Apostle says in I Cor. 1[:21], "For since, in the wisdom of God, the world did not know God through wisdom, it pleased God through the folly of what we preach to save those who believe." Now it is not sufficient for

1. LW 31:48–49; WA 1:359.32–360.4.

anyone, and it does him no good to recognize God in his glory and majesty, unless he recognizes him in the humility and shame of the cross. Thus God destroys the wisdom of the wise, as Isa. [45:15] says, "Truly, thou art a God who hidest thyself."

So, also, in John 14[:8], where Philip spoke according to the theology of glory: "Show us the Father." Christ forthwith set aside his flighty thought about seeking God elsewhere and led him to himself, saying, "Philip, he who has seen me has seen the Father" [John 14:9]. For this reason true theology and recognition of God are in the crucified Christ, as it is also stated in John 10 [John 14:6]: "No one comes to the Father, but by me." "I am the door" [John 10:9], and so forth.

21. *A theologian of glory calls evil good and good evil. A theologian of the cross calls the thing what it actually is.*

This is clear: He who does not know Christ does not know God hidden in suffering. Therefore he prefers works to suffering, glory to the cross, strength to weakness, wisdom to folly, and, in general, good to evil. These are the people whom the apostle calls "enemies of the cross of Christ" [Phil. 3:18], for they hate the cross and suffering and love works and the glory of works. Thus they call the good of the cross evil and the evil of a deed good. God can be found only in suffering and the cross, as has already been said. Therefore the friends of the cross say that the cross is good and works are evil, for through the cross works are destroyed and the old Adam, who is especially edified by works, is crucified. It is impossible for a person not to be puffed up by his good works unless he has first been deflated and destroyed by suffering and evil until he knows that he is worthless and that his works are not his but God's.[2]

23. *The law brings the wrath of God, kills, reviles, accuses, judges, and condemns everything that is not in Christ [Rom. 4:15].*

Thus Gal. 3[:18] states, "Christ redeemed us from the curse of the law"; and: "For all who rely on works of the law are under the curse" [Gal. 3:10]; and Rom. 4 [15]: "For the law brings wrath"; and Rom. 7[:10]: "The very commandment which promised life proved to be the death of me"; Rom. 2[:12]: "All who have sinned without the law will also perish without law." Therefore he who boasts that he is wise and learned in the law boasts in his confusion, his damnation, the wrath of God, in death. As Rom. 2[:23] puts it: "You who boast in the law."[3]

25. *He is not righteous who does much, but he who, without work, believes much in Christ.*

---

2. LW 31:52–53; WA 1:361.31–362.33.
3. LW 31:54–55; WA 1:363.15–24.

For the righteousness of God is not acquired by means of acts frequently repeated, as Aristotle taught, but it is imparted by faith, for "He who through faith is righteous shall live" (Rom. 1[:17]), and "Man believes with his heart and so is justified" (Rom. 10[:10]). Therefore I wish to have the words "without work" understood in the following manner: Not that the righteous person does nothing, but that his works do not make him righteous, rather that his righteousness creates works. For grace and faith are infused without our works. After they have been imparted the works follow. Thus Rom. 3[:20] states, "No human being will be justified in His sight by works of the law," and, "For we hold that man is justified by faith apart from works of law" (Rom. 3[:28]). In other words, works contribute nothing to justification. Therefore man knows that works which he does by such faith are not his but God's. For this reason he does not seek to become justified or glorified through them, but seeks God. His justification by faith in Christ is sufficient to him. Christ is his wisdom, righteousness, etc., as I Cor. 1[:30] has it, that he himself may be Christ's action and instrument.

26. *The law says, "do this," and it is never done. Grace says, "believe in this," and everything is already done.*

The first part is clear from what has been stated by the Apostle and his interpreter, St. Augustine, in many places. And it has been stated often enough above that the law works wrath and keeps all men under the curse. The second part is clear from the same sources, for faith justifies. "And the law (says St. Augustine) commands what faith obtains." For through faith Christ is in us, indeed, one with us. Christ is just and has fulfilled all the commands of God, wherefore we also fulfill everything through him since he was made ours through faith.[4]

28. *The love of God does not find, but creates, that which is pleasing to it. The love of man comes into being through that which is pleasing to it.*

The second part is clear and is accepted by all philosophers and theologians, for the object of love is its cause, assuming, according to Aristotle, that all power of the soul is passive and material and active only in receiving something. Thus it is also demonstrated that Aristotle's philosophy is contrary to theology since in all things it seeks those things which are its own and receives rather than gives something good. The first part is clear because the love of God which lives in man loves sinners, evil persons, fools, and weaklings in order to make them righteous, good, wise, and strong. Rather than seeking its own good, the love of God flows forth and bestows good. Therefore sinners are attractive because they are loved; they are not loved because they are attractive. For this reason the love of man avoids sinners

---

4. LW 31:55–56; WA 1:364.1–26.

and evil persons. Thus Christ says: "For I came not to call the righteous, but sinners" [Matt. 9:13]. This is the love of the cross, born of the cross, which turns in the direction where it does not find good which it may enjoy, but where it may confer good upon the bad and needy person. "It is more blessed to give than to receive" [Acts 20:35], says the Apostle. Hence Ps. 41[:1] states, "Blessed is he who considers the poor," for the intellect cannot by nature comprehend an object which does not exist, that is the poor and needy person, but only a thing which does exist, that is the true and good. Therefore it judges according to appearances, is a respecter of persons, and judges according to that which can be seen, etc.[5]

COMMENTARY: TAKEN FROM GERHARD FORDE'S BOOK, ON BEING A THEOLOGIAN OF THE CROSS: REFLECTIONS ON LUTHER'S HEIDELBERG DISPUTATION, 1518 (GRAND RAPIDS: EERDMANS, 1997).

The Disputation is set up quite consistently as a series of sharp contrasts— or better, antitheses—between the two ways of being theologians and the stories that lie behind them. The antitheses focus on the basic issue of salvation: the question of law and works; the power of the human will; the attempt to "see" God; the task of speaking the truth in these matters; faith; and ultimately of the love of God, which creates its own object. The argument proceeds by constantly setting the way of glory over against the way of the cross. In every instance all loopholes are closed so that the believer will in the end simply be cast on the creative love of God, which makes the object of its love out of the nothing to which the sinner has been reduced.

The Disputation itself, one might say, illustrates the manner in which theologians of the cross operate. Claimed, that is to say killed and made alive by the cross alone as *the* story, theologians of the cross attack the way of glory, the way of law, human works, and free will, because the way of glory simply operates as a defense mechanism against the cross. Theologians of glory operate with fundamentally different presuppositions about how one comes to know God. They think one can see *through* the created world and the acts of God to the invisible realm of glory beyond it, and they must think this because for the system to work there must be a "glory road," a way of law, which the fallen creature can traverse by willing and working and thus gain the necessary merit eventually to arrive at glory.

---

5. LW 31:57–58; WA 1:365.1–20.

The cross too is transparent. The theologian of glory sees through the cross so as to fit it into the scheme of works. The cross "makes up" for failures along the glory road. The upshot of it all is a fundamental misreading of reality. The theologian of glory ends up by calling evil good and good evil. Works are good and suffering is evil. The God who presides over this enterprise must therefore be excused from all blame for what was termed "evil." The theology of glory ends in a simplistic understanding of God. God, according to philosophers like Plato, is not the cause of all things but only what we might call "good." It is hard to see how such a god could even be involved in the cross.

Theologians of the cross, however, "say what a thing is." That is, a characteristic mark of theologians of the cross is that they learn to call a spade a spade. Since the cross story alone is their story, they are not driven by the attempt to see through it, but are drawn into the story. They know that faith means to live *in* the Christ of the story. Likewise they do not believe that we come to proper knowledge of God by attempting to see through the created world to the "invisible things of God." So theologians of the cross look on all things "through suffering and the cross." They, in other words, are led by the cross to *look at* the trials, the sufferings, the pangs of conscience, the troubles—and joys—of daily life as God's doing and do not try to *see through* them as mere accidental problems to be solved by metaphysical adjustment. They are not driven to simplistic theodicies because with St. Paul they believe that God justifies himself precisely in the cross and resurrection of Jesus. They know that, dying to the old, the believer lives *in* Christ and looks forward to being raised with him.

Theologians of the cross therefore come to understand that the only move left is to the proclamation that issues from the story. The final task is to *do* the story to the hearers in such a way that they are incorporated into the story itself, killed and made alive by the hearing of it. The hearers are claimed by the story. Thus theologians of the cross will be compelled to theologize on the story that there are no escape hatches, no loopholes. They are constrained to rule out the attempt to see through creation or the cross to some supposed secret behind it. There is no secret passage to glory. They insist that there is no other place to look but to the cross story itself. This means that a certain suspicion and polemical edge is usually evident. Theologians of the cross know the temptations of a theology of glory well and are concerned to counter them at every turn. In essence, that is what comes to expression in Luther's Heidelberg Disputation. It is a thoroughgoing exposition and refutation of a theology of glory.[6]

6. Gerhard O. Forde, *On Being A Theologian of the Cross: Reflections on Luther's*

On Thesis 28

Here we have reached the other side. God is not, as in the theology of glory, one who waits to approve those who have improved themselves, made themselves acceptable, or merited approval, but one who *bestows* good on the bad and needy. The great reversal is complete. Indeed, the final sentences of the proof touch in interesting fashion on a reversal in the very question of being itself. *[. . .Forde here quotes the end of Luther's explanation of Thesis 28, given above].*

The problem is that for a theology of glory the bad, poor, needy, or lowly cannot really exist. What really exists is the true, the good, and the beautiful, the great abstractions, the "invisible" things of God. Because the theologian of glory is always looking through what is actually given, the bad, poor, needy, and lowly are invisible. They don't show up on the scale of values and are not regarded. "Evil" is nonbeing. God has nothing to do with it. Hence, there is no reason why the Lord of all should condescend to them. But the Psalmist sees it otherwise, "Blessed is he who considers the poor."

Here at last the existential situation of the fallen creature, the sinfulness and need for salvation, is equated with the very question of being itself. We get further insight into what it means to look on all things through suffering and the cross. Whereas the theologian of glory tries to see through the needy, the poor, the lowly, and the "nonexistent," the theologian of the cross knows that the love of God creates precisely out of nothing. Therefore the sinner must be reduced to nothing in order to be saved. The presupposition of the entire Disputation is laid bare. It is the hope of the resurrection. God brings life out of death. He calls into being that which is from that which is not. In order that there be a resurrection, the sinner must die. All presumption must be ended. The truth must be seen. Only the "friends of the cross" who have been reduced to nothing are properly prepared to receive the justifying grace poured out by the creative love of God. All other roads are closed. The theologian of the cross is thus one who finally is turned about to see "the way things are."[7]

FURTHER READING

Brecht, Martin. *Martin Luther: His Road to Reformation, 1481–1521.* Translated by James L. Schaff. Minneapolis: Fortress, 1985, 215–16, 231–35.

Heidelberg Disputation, 1518 (Grand Rapids: Eerdmans, 1997), 12–14.

7. Forde, *On Being a Theologian of the Cross*, 113–15.

Forde, Gerhard O. *On Being a Theologian of the Cross: Reflections on Luther's Heidelberg Disputation, 1518.* Grand Rapids: Eerdmans, 1997.

Kittelson, James. *Luther the Reformer: The Story of the Man and His Career.* Minneapolis: Augsburg, 1986, 111–14.

Leppin, Volker. *Martin Luther: Gestalten des Mittelalters und der Renaissance.* Darmstadt: Wissenschaftliche Buchgesellschaft, 2006, 126–35.

Wengert, Timothy J., ed. *The Annotated Luther, Volume 1: The Roots of Reform.* Minneapolis: Fortress, 2015, 67–120.

3

The Diet of Augsburg (1518)

SUZANNE HEQUET

MARTIN LUTHER'S WRITING OF the 95 *Theses* in 1517 has been celebrated this past year as the five-hundredth anniversary of the event that sparked the Reformation. Still, 2018 marks an opportunity to focus on another key moment that defined the early Reformation. Specifically, in 1518 Luther faced a papal legate, Cardinal Cajetan, in meetings held during an imperial diet in Augsburg. The 500th anniversary of this meeting lifted up Luther's arguments on the nature of faith and certainty—arguments that shook Cajetan's Thomist theology, and thereby exposed papal authority as the crux of issues surrounding reform.

In 1517 Luther's academic dispute over indulgences, which began with the distribution of the 95 *Theses* on 31 October, was followed by two kinds of attacks. To begin with, theologians north of the Alps, such as Johann Tetzel and Conrad Wimpina, issued counter-theses and arguments. When Archbishop Albrecht of Mainz sent the *Theses* to Rome, however, the academic dispute automatically became an ecclesiastical case, perhaps expanded by a separate brief by Dominicans like Tetzel. First to answer Luther's *Theses* in Rome was the papal court theologian, Silvester Prierias, who in July 1518 published the *Dialogus*, in which he argued that Luther misunderstood his own presuppositions and needed especially to understand papal authority.

This publication was an important first step in the papal decision to initiate formal proceedings against Luther.[1]

Meanwhile, by May 1518, Luther had written a defense of the 95 *Theses*, the *Explanations of the Ninety-Five Theses*, dedicated to Pope Leo X and authorized for publication by Luther's ordinary, the bishop of Brandenburg, but not published until August.[2] By the end of August, following a meeting of the German chapter of the Augustinian Order in April 1518, Luther published his response to Prierias, insisting on a coalition of authorities that he would later use in his encounter with Cajetan: reason, the fathers of the church, the official church decrees (canon law) and, above all, the Bible.

In the summer of 1518 an imperial diet convened in Augsburg, to which the pope sent his legate, Cardinal Cajetan (also known as Tommaso de Vio). Already on 7 August Luther had received a summons to face trial in Rome. Matters had moved beyond learned debate to something far more serious, and Luther did not hide his alarm. To complicate matters, during Lent 1518 Luther had delivered a sermon on excommunication and its abuse by church authorities. Opponents had composed a distorted set of theses on the subject under Luther's name and circulated them at the diet.[3] The emperor Maximilian was outraged and called for action. On 23 August the pope delivered to Cajetan a summons that Luther appear in Rome to answer charges of heresy. On 11 September Cajetan received permission to interrogate Luther in Augsburg and either receive his recantation or condemn him. The pope also sent word to Luther's prince, Elector Frederick, to assist in an arrest, if such action was necessary.[4] Frederick delayed a few weeks, but then, in a shrewd political move, requested that Luther appear in Augsburg in late September under a letter of safe conduct. Thus, in early October, Luther set out for Augsburg. En route, he was joined in Nuremberg by Wenceslas Linck, a fellow Augustinian.

At Augsburg the proceedings between Luther and Cajetan consisted of three meetings from 11–14 October 1518. Having received his letter of safe conduct for travel in the city of Augsburg, Luther met with the Cardinal for

1. Perhaps as early as June 1518, a summons had been prepared for Luther to appear in Rome within sixty days. For the historical reconstruction here, see Martin Brecht, *Martin Luther: His Road to Reformation, 1483–1521*, trans. James L. Schaaf (Minneapolis: Fortress, 1985), 239–65.

2. LW 31:77–252. This defense also contained a prefatory letter to Johann von Staupitz, the head of the Augustinian Order in Germany, printed in LW 48:64–70. For the letter to Leo X, see WA 1:527–29. The full defense is found at WA 1:529–628.

3. Luther responded by publishing his own Latin version of the *Sermon on the Ban* (August 1518), LW 39:3–22.

4. For this letter, see Preserved Smith, ed., *Luther's Correspondence and Other Contemporary Letters*, vol. 1 (Philadelphia: Lutheran Publication Society, 1913), 105–6.

the first time on 12 October. In the following text, written after he returned to Wittenberg on 31 October 1518, Luther recounted his meetings with Cajetan at Augsburg.

THE PROCEEDINGS OF FRIAR MARTIN LUTHER, AUGUSTINIAN, WITH THE LORD APOSTOLIC LEGATE AT AUGSBURG[5]

To the Godly Reader, Friar Martin Luther Extends Greetings

Now, dear reader, what I am doing is this: I see that pamphlets are being published and various rumors are being spread concerning my activities at Augsburg, although I really accomplished nothing more there than the loss of time and money. Probably, however, it was enough of an accomplishment to have heard a new Latin language, namely, that teaching the truth is the same as confusing the church—indeed, that flattering and also denying Christ would be equivalent to pacifying and exalting the church of Christ. For I do not see how you could but appear to be a barbarian to the Romans and the Romans barbarians to you if you did not master this kind of eloquence, even if you were to surpass the eloquence of Cicero. Therefore, to avoid extremes, so that friends of my cause do not excessively elevate it or enemies excessively lower it, I wish to make public the charges against me and my answers to them.

By this testimony I wish to make it known that I excelled in giving the Roman pontiff exceptional and faithful obedience. In the first place, I, poor and weak though I am, set out on foot on a long journey, thus exposing myself to dangers, and I did not take advantage of just and honorable excuses for staying away, which all would have judged acceptable. In the second place, I appeared before those whom I could have refused to see, because they belonged on the side of my enemies. However, it seems to me (were I to follow my nose) that these so-called friends have contrived these evil and troublesome conditions and have arranged all matters so that they would more readily contribute to my destruction and not to the search for truth. Nor does it seem as though they expected me to come but hoped that

5. Included here are sections of a new translation of the "Proceedings at Augsburg, 1518" by Suzanne Hequet. This was originally printed in AL 121–65. This translation of the *Acta Augustana 1518* is a revision of that by Harold J. Grimm in LW 31:253–92 based upon WA 2:1–26. The tract was titled: *Acta F. Martini Luther Augustiniani apud D. Legatum Apostolicum Augustae* (Wittenberg: Grunenberg, 1518).

I would obstinately refuse to come so that they could inflict the punishment without a hearing and secretly triumph over me. The not insignificant proof of this I gathered from the fact that the question of the accusation against me was not raised until after my arrival. And up to the present day my writings are in the house of Caiaphas, where they seek false testimony against me and have not yet found it.[6] So this new custom (as I see it) or new law of the Roman Curia has been initiated to first seize Christ and then to look for a charge against him. Nevertheless, I have been accused of two things—really only one—which has the appearance of an accusation, that is, my statement concerning the *Extravagante*,[7] as you will presently learn.[8]

Luther next recounted events leading up to his first meeting with the cardinal, followed by an account of the first meeting itself. Cajetan stated he did not want to argue with Luther, but the pope demanded responses to three points: that Luther recant his errors, promise to abstain from such errors in the future, and that he avoid doing anything in the future that might disturb the church. Luther asked for specifics on his errors, so that he could avoid such mistakes in the future. Cajetan referenced a lesser-known papal bull of 1343, Clement VI's *Unigenitus*. But Luther knew that bull well, noting it was commonly called it *Extravagante*. Cajetan again called for Luther to recant, but following Luther's refusal, Cajetan moved to a second point. In Luther's explanation of thesis 7 in his 95 *Theses*, the cardinal objected to Luther's assertion that a person taking the sacrament of the Lord's Supper must have faith, or the sacrament would be taken to the person's damnation. Luther countered that the *Extrangante* was not based on scripture, yet his thesis 7 was clearly supported in scripture. At this point, Cajetan moved to assert papal authority, saying it was above church councils, scripture, and the entire church. Luther denied papal authority and asked for time to think. Thus ended the first meeting.

Luther testified formally the next day in the presence of four counselors for the emperor, while he had with him a notary and witnesses. Having declared that he had cherished the Roman church in all his words, Luther read from his prepared text. He began by stating that he, an Augustinian,

---

6. An analogy to Jesus' trial in Matthew 26:57–68 and his appearance before the High Priest Caiaphas.

7. 1343 *Unigenitus*, papal bull of Clement VI, called *Extravagante* (literally something wandering about) because it was included in an appendix, rather than in the main body of Gratian's *Decretum*.

8. See AL 129–30.

cherished the holy Roman church. Still, Luther could not comply with the three orders Cajetan had leveled the previous day. In Luther's words:

> Today I declare publicly that I am not conscious of having said anything contrary to Holy Scripture, the church fathers, the papal decretals or right reason. All that I have said today seems to me to have been sensible, true, and catholic. Nevertheless, since I am a man who can err, I have submitted and now again submit to the judgment and the lawful decision of the holy church and of all who are better informed than I. In addition to this, however, I offer myself personally here or elsewhere to give an account also in public of all that I have said. But if this does not please the most reverend lord legate, I am even prepared to answer in writing the objections which he intends to raise against me, and to hear the judgment and opinion concerning these points of the doctors of the famed imperial universities of Basel, Freiburg, and Louvain, or, if this is not satisfactory, also of Paris, the parent of learning and from the beginning the university which was most Christian and most renowned in theology.[9]

Cajetan responded by insisting again that Luther recant. Luther was silent at first, but then promised to respond in writing the following day. So ended the second meeting between the two.

In Luther's written response, presented the following day on 14 October 1518, Luther began by again objecting to the *Unigenitus*, noting "Furthermore, it occurred to me that the *Unigenitus* twists the words of Scripture and abuses them by giving them another meaning, for what was said [in scripture] concerning justifying grace it applies to indulgences."[10] Luther followed with more condemnations, then gave examples of how scripture had been twisted.

> Furthermore, it also disquieted me that it could quite possibly happen that papal decretals occasionally are erroneous and militate against Holy Scriptures and charity. For if one ought to obey the papal decretals as though they were the voice of St. Peter, as it is stated in *distinctio* XIX, still this is to be understood only of those decretals that are in agreement with Holy Scripture and the decretals of previous popes, as stated in the same authority. Add to this the fact that Peter, when not walking in the truth of the gospel, is actually reprimanded by Paul in Gal. 2[:14]. Therefore it does not appear strange if his successor has erred in some

9. See AL 133–34.
10. See AL 136.

point or other, since indeed it is stated in Acts 15[:1–19] that the teaching of Peter was not accepted until it had been accepted and approved by James the Younger, the bishop of Jerusalem, and agreed to by the entire church. From this seems to have arisen the legal principle that a law becomes established only when it is approved by those living according to its regulations.[11]

As Luther remained convinced that his theses were correctly stated, he next listed seven specific points, in which he attempted to show how his theses might be in agreement with the *Unigenitus*, thereby, hopefully, preserving the truth of both.[12] He ended this list of objections with the following:

> Briefly, if the *Extravagante* is to be retained as authoritative, it is thus clear that the merits of Christ must of necessity be understood in a twofold sense. On the one hand, according to the literal and formal sense, the merits of Christ are a treasure of the life-giving Spirit. Since they are his very own, the Holy Spirit apportions them to whomever he wills. On the other hand, according to the non-literal, effective sense, they only signify, according to the letter and the incidental consequences, a treasure created by the merits of Christ. And as the *Extravagante* quotes the Scriptures in a non-literal sense, so also it understands the treasure, the merits of Christ, and all other concepts, in a non-literal sense. For this reason, it is ambiguous and obscure, and affords a most proper occasion for debate. In my theses, on the other hand, I spoke in terms of the proper sense [of treasure]. Whoever has a better understanding of this, let him give it to me, and I will recant [my understanding], for it is not my duty to interpret the canons of the popes but to defend my theses, lest they may seem to be in opposition to the canons. In humility I expect that, if the pope is of a different mind, he will let it be known, and I am willing to comply.[13]

Luther next turned to objections that Cajetan had brought against thesis 7.[14] In Luther's words:

> This I answer by saying: 1. It is an infallible truth that no person is righteous unless such a person believes in God, as stated in Rom. 1[:17]: "The one who through faith is righteous shall live." Likewise [John 3:18], "The one who does not believe is

11. See AL 136.

12. See AL 138–40.

13. See AL 140–41.

14. Luther, *Explanations*, LW 31:98.

condemned already" and dead. Therefore the justification and life of the righteous person are dependent upon his or her faith. For this reason all the works of the believer are alive and all the works of the unbeliever are dead, evil, and damnable, as in this passage [Matt. 7:18–19]: "A bad tree cannot bear good fruit. Every tree that does not bear good fruit is cut down and thrown into the fire."

2. Faith, however, is nothing more than believing what God promises and reveals, as in Rom. 4[:3], "Abraham believed God, and he reckoned it to him as righteousness."[15] Therefore the Word and faith are both necessary, and without the Word there can be no faith, as in Isa. 55[:11]: "So shall my word be that goes forth from my mouth; it shall not return to me empty."

3. I must now prove that those going to the sacrament must believe that they will receive grace, and not doubt it, but rather have absolute confidence. Otherwise they will receive the sacrament to their condemnation.[16]

Luther followed with eleven more points in support of these positions. Finally, he summarized Cajetan's response to the submitted statement as follows:

When I presented Cajetan with the above statement the next day, he at first considered it worthless and said that it consisted of mere words. But then he said that he would send it to Rome. Meanwhile he insisted that I recant, threatening me with the punishments that had been recommended to him, and he said that if I did not recant, I should leave him and stay out of his sight. When I heard this and realized that he was firm in his position and would not consider the Scripture passages, and since I had also determined I would not recant, I left, with no hope of returning. Even though he said and now still boasts that he would have acted toward me as a father and not as a judge, I could not detect any such paternal attitude, except one that was sterner than any court of justice. All he did was demand that I recant against my conscience. At least he did not show a desire or the ability to demonstrate to me where I was wrong or to convince me of my error, for when he saw that I rejected the comments of the opinionated scholastics, he promised to take action against me on the basis of Holy Scripture and canon law. What he meant by this, I do not know, for he never produced a syllable from the Holy Scriptures against me, and to

15. Gen. 15:6.

16. See AL 141–42.

the present day he could not do so, even if he were to put forth a special effort, since there is universal agreement that nothing in the Holy Scriptures mentions indulgences. On the contrary, the Scriptures commend faith and are as devoid of references to indulgences as they are full of teaching concerning faith, so that it is impossible for the legate thereby to demolish either one of these two articles.[17]

Luther continued to defend his refusal to recant, but was ordered to leave the presence of the cardinal. Cajetan then called upon Staupitz, urging him to appeal to Luther, an appeal that did not work. Luther remained another two days, upon which he sent a letter to Cajetan. Nothing happened. Finally, Luther was urged by friends to leave Augsburg, which he did. In a final note, Luther reiterated to his readers that he presented his last response "with great reverence,"[18] submitting it also to the judgment of the pope. Following Luther's comments, the legal brief from Pope Leo X to Cardinal Cajetan was included. Luther closed with his own thoughts on the papal brief in the final section of this writing to his dear reader.

COMMENTARY

Cajetan had been ordered via a papal communiqué to avoid debate with Luther and simply to demand his recantation, but both theologians were soon drawn into the fray.[19] Both Luther's legal representative and Johann von Staupitz, the head of the Augustinian order in Germany, accompanied him to the first meeting, where Cajetan, contrary to the papal instructions, was drawn into debate with Luther.

In that first interview, the longest of the three, Cajetan raised questions on two fronts: challenging thesis 58 of the 95 *Theses* and the arguments on thesis 7 in Luther's *Explanations of the Ninety-five Theses*.[20] Cajetan defended papal authority to sell indulgences as based on the Gospel text, John 20:23, and on a papal decree of Clement VI not found in all collections of canon law. He assumed that, because of this, Luther would not be familiar with the decree. Luther was indeed aware of this decree but argued that on the higher authority of scripture it should be rescinded. The objections raised to Luther's arguments defending thesis 7 touched upon the heart of justification

---

17. That is, Cajetan's objections to thesis 58 and the explanation to thesis 7. For full text of this section, see AL 147–49.

18. AL 150.

19. Brecht, 1:250.

20. For entire *Explanations*, see WA 1:525–628. For thesis 7 see LW 31:98–107.

by faith: whether in private confession a person could completely trust the priest's absolution (namely, God's promise of forgiveness). Cajetan argued, based upon his Augustinian understanding of true humility, that a person should never be certain of his or her standing before God. For Luther, the certainty of God's promise outweighed any doubts, which in any case could not be made the basis for one's relation to God.

In these early discussions, most of Luther's opponents were firm supporters of papal authority. Whereas Luther was an Augustinian friar trained in Nominalism, several of his opponents were members of the Dominican order and embraced an Augustinian theology seen through the lens of Thomas Aquinas's theology, a theology that by the sixteenth century routinely defended papal authority in matters of doctrine and practice.[21] Cajetan's line of questioning, which the Italian Thomist had prepared from a careful reading of Luther's work, was designed to convince Luther of the error of his position on indulgences and church authority.

On the second day, Luther was accompanied again by Staupitz, together with four imperial counselors. Luther requested a public hearing, a request Cajetan denied. Luther then insisted on reading a written statement in response to Cajetan's points raised at their first meeting and asked permission to defend himself and to be judged by theologians at one of the universities in Louvain, Basel, Freiburg, or Paris. This request was also denied.

At the third and final meeting, two lawyers from Frederick's court accompanied Luther. He presented a written statement and made three key points. First, a general church council held authority over the pope. Second, a sacrament given to an unbeliever imparted no grace. Third, the doctrine of justification by faith, supported throughout scripture, was key to understanding the proper meaning of penance and indulgences. After some hesitation, Cajetan accepted the statement and agreed to send it to the pope along with his refutation. But by now, Cajetan was clearly angered. He asked Luther to recant or leave his presence immediately and not return. Luther simply left without recanting.

Luther wrote a letter of apology, again asking for specifics on where he erred, but he received no reply.[22] Hearing that Luther would be arrested, Staupitz released Luther from his monastic vows and advised him to return to Wittenberg. Before leaving Augsburg, Luther officially appealed Cajetan's decision to Pope Leo X by having his appeal posted on the cathedral door in

21. For these early opponents, see David V. N. Bagchi, *Luther's Earliest Opponents: Catholic Controversialists, 1518–1525* (Minneapolis: Fortress, 1991), 23; and Scott H. Hendrix, *Luther and the Papacy: Stages in a Reformation Conflict* (Philadelphia: Fortress, 1981), 46–52.

22. See LW 48:87–89.

Augsburg.[23] A month later, when the pope reiterated his support for indulgences, Luther appealed for the first time to a general council. For those who defended the primacy of papal authority over any council, however, this was simply a further indication of Luther's heresy. Once back in Wittenberg, Luther wrote his account of these events in his *Proceedings at Augsburg, 1518*, which was published in early December 1518.

These proceedings marked a watershed in the Reformation. The very methods of argumentation employed by Cajetan and later by John Eck at the 1519 Leipzig debates pushed matters beyond simple academic debate and toward a full-blown break in the church over questions of authority.[24] Perhaps even more importantly, the arguments over the nature of faith and certainty indicated a shift in thinking that went far beyond the medieval theology of humility and centered instead in the sure and certain word of Christ and faith in that word. Whether this also implied a new human self-understanding in Western thought is still a matter of debate.[25]

FURTHER READING

Brecht, Martin. *Martin Luther: His Road to Reformation, 1481–1521*. Translated by James L. Schaff. Philadelphia: Fortress, 1985, 231–65.

Hendrix, Scott H. *Luther and the Papacy: Stages in a Reformation Conflict*. Philadelphia: Fortress, 1981, 51–70.

Kittelson, James M., and Hans H. Wiersma. *Luther the Reformer: The Story of the Man and His Career, Second Edition*. Minneapolis: Fortress, 2016, 81–92.

Spehr, Christopher. *Luther und das Konzil: Zur Entwicklung eines zentralen Themas in der Reformationszeit*. Tübingen: Mohr/Siebeck, 2010, 61–75 and 91–91.

Wengert, Timothy J., ed. *The Annotated Luther*, Vol. 1: *The Roots of Reform*. Minneapolis: Fortress, 2015, 121–65.

23. See Christopher Spehr, *Luther und das Konzil: zur Entwicklung eines zentralen Themas in der Reformationszeit* (Tübingen: Mohr/Siebeck, 2010), 91.

24. See Brecht, 1:264–65, 317–22.

25. Otto H. Pesch, "'Das heisst eine neue Kirche bauen': Luther und Cajetan in Augsburg" in: *Begegnung: Beiträge zu einer Hermeneutik des theologischen Gesprächs*, ed. Otto Pesch et al. (Graz: Styria, 1972), 660.

4

The Leipzig Debate (1519)

KURT K. HENDEL

THE 95 THESES[1] SWIFTLY brought Martin Luther (1481–1546) to the attention of the contemporary ecclesiastical and political leadership and of the general public. In the *Theses* Luther attacked the sale of indulgences and raised questions regarding the whole penitential system of the church. The *Theses* thus not only challenged the church's theology and piety, but they also quickly affected one of its major sources of income. The church's response to the dissemination of the *Theses* was, therefore, a quick one. The Dominicans initially led that response, but other defenders of the church also raised their voices in opposition to Luther. One of the most capable and persistent Roman apologists was Johannes Eck (1481–1543).

Eck and Luther carried on a friendly correspondence in 1517, most likely because both had been influenced by Humanism and sought to address abuses within the church and to promote reform. However, Eck was not inclined to challenge the authority of the papacy and of the church in general and decided to voice his opposition to the *95 Theses* by preparing a written critique in 1518, which he titled *Obelisks*. While he initially intended the document to circulate privately, it was leaked and printed. The work reached Wittenberg in March of 1518. Luther was surprised and disappointed that his collegial correspondent had chosen to attack him,

---

1. LW 31:16–33.

and he responded with his *Asterisks*.[2] Andreas Bodenstein von Karlstadt (1481–1541), Luther's colleague in Wittenberg, believed that the *Obelisks* were an attack on his theology and vision of reform as well as Luther's, and he was determined to defend himself, the whole Wittenberg faculty, and Luther against Eck's critique. He, therefore, published 370 and ultimately 405 Theses[3] in defense of the Wittenbergers. Eck wrote to Karlstadt expressing surprise that the latter had attacked him,[4] and Karlstadt responded by offering his friendship, if Eck decided to be a lover of truth.[5] Rather than meeting Karlstadt's demand, Eck responded with his *Defense*,[6] which inspired Karlstadt to produce his own *Defense*[7] in September of 1518. Karlstadt also noted that he was willing to engage Eck in a public debate if his expenses were refunded, he was given a safe conduct, and notaries were appointed to record the debate.[8]

Luther met Eck personally in Augsburg in October 1518. Luther had been summoned to Augsburg in order to meet with the papal legate, Thomas Cardinal Cajetan (1461–1534), but Eck also happened to be in the city at the same time.[9] During their chance meeting, Luther and Eck discussed the anticipated debate between Eck and Karlstadt and potential places where it might be held, namely, Erfurt or Leipzig. Luther reported this conversation to Karlstadt, and, in a letter to Eck, Karlstadt informed the Ingolstadt professor that he should choose the site.[10] Leipzig was chosen,

---

2. WA 1:278–314. The *Asterisks* include quotations from Eck's *Obelisks*. For a German translation of the *Asterisks* see SLE 18: cols. 536–89.

3. See SLE 18, cols. 590–633 for a German translation of the Theses.

4. Eck's letter is entry 84 (May 28, 1518) in *Kritische Gesamtausgabe der Schriften und Briefe Andreas Bodensteins von Karlstadt*, Teil I (1507–1518), ed. by Thomas Kaufmann, Wolfenbütteler Digitale Bibliothek (Wolfenbüttel: Herzog August Bibliothek, 2012). Hereafter referred to as Kaufmann, *Karlstadt*.

5. Karlstadt's letter is entry 86 (June 11, 1518) in Kaufmann, *Karlstadt*.

6. *Defensio Joannis Eckii contra amarulentas D. Andreae Bodenstein Carolstatini invectiones* (*Defense of Johannes Eck against the bitter invectives of Dr. Andreas Bodenstein von Karlstadt*). See *Corpus Catholicum. Werke katholischer Schriftsteller im Zeitalter der Glaubensspaltung*, vol. 1, ed. by Joseph Greving (Münster: Aschendorffsch, 1919).

7. *Defensio Andreae Carolostadii adversus eximii D. Ioannis Eckii . . . monomachiam* (*The Defense of Andreas Karlstadt against the Monomachy of the excellent Dr. Johannes Eck*). The *Defensio* is entry 90 in Kaufmann, *Karlstadt*. For a German translation of the treatise see SLE 18, cols. 632–711.

8. W.H.T. Dau, *The Leipzig Debate in 1519: Leaves from the Story of Luther's Life* (St. Louis: Concordia Publishing House, 1919), 40. Hereafter cited as Dau.

9. See the previous installment in this series about quincentennials, namely, Suzanne Hequet, "The 1518 Proceedings at Augsburg," *Lutheran Quarterly* 32 (2018): 60–70.

10. Dau, 43–45.

no doubt because Eck was aware that the University and Duke George of Saxony (1471–1539) were supportive of his defense of the church, its theology, and its practices. The next preparatory step for the debate was to secure a commitment from the University and from the Duke to host the debate. This goal was accomplished after negotiations between the Duke and the theological faculty of Leipzig; Duke George and the university therefore issued an invitation to Eck and Karlstadt. It was also decided that June 27, 1519, would be the starting date and that the Universities of Erfurt and Paris would be asked to judge the results of the debate.

Eck sought to clarify the agenda for the debate by publishing twelve theses in December 1518 that dealt with indulgences, purgatory, and penance but also introduced an additional topic for debate, namely, papal authority. In preparing the twelve theses, Eck was responding directly to Luther's *Explanation of the Ninety-five Theses*,[11] particularly to the Reformer's comments regarding thesis 22 in which Luther had addressed Rome's authority but without giving it much attention.[12] Eck's theses were another indicator that he was interested in debating Luther much more than Karlstadt. Luther published twelve theses of his own in response to Eck's theses. The twelve theses of Eck and of Luther were expanded to thirteen shortly before the debate when Eck added a thesis defending the freedom of the will[13] and Luther responded to Eck by adding a thesis rejecting free will and emphasizing the necessity of faith. Luther included his thirteen theses in his *Disputation and Defense of Brother Martin Luther against the Accusations of Dr. Johann Eck*.[14] The theses summarized the theological perspectives that Luther would ultimately rearticulate and defend at the Leipzig Debate.

Luther was obviously a participant in the literary jousting that served as the immediate context of and impetus for the Leipzig Debate. He also hoped that he would be allowed to travel to Leipzig and receive permission from Duke George to participate in the debate. It was not clear, however, that such permission would be granted. The Duke had only invited Eck and Karlstadt to debate in Leipzig and had also promised a safe conduct to Karlstadt and his companions.[15] While he did not specifically exclude

11. LW 31:77–252. See also WA 1:522–628.

12. In his *Explanations of the Ninety-Five Theses,* specifically of thesis 22, Luther asserted that during the time of Pope Gregory I (c. 540–604) the Roman church "had no jurisdiction over other churches, at least not over the Greek church." LW 31:152; WA 1:571.

13. See SLE 18, cols. 712–15 for a German translation of Eck's thirteen theses.

14. LW 31:313–318. The Latin title of the work was *Disputatio et excusatio F. Martini Luther adversus criminationes D. Johannis Eckii.* See WA 2:153–61.

15. The safe conduct, which was issued on June 10, read: "At the desire of Dr.

Luther as a potential member of the Wittenberg contingent, he did not give him explicit permission to join the debate or assure him of a personal safe conduct. Therefore, Luther addressed several letters to the Duke requesting that he be allowed to debate as well, but explicit permission was not granted until after the debate had begun and Eck had clarified that he desired to debate Luther.

THE DEBATE

The Leipzig Debate was carried on in three stages from June 27-July 16, 1519.[16] From June 27 until July 3, Eck and Karlstadt explored whether God's grace alone or grace and human free will inspire believers to do good works. Eck defended the latter option, while Karlstadt rejected Eck's synergistic position and emphasized the exclusive necessity of grace. Luther and Eck debated from the morning of July 4 until the early morning of July 14[17] and focused particularly on papal authority and the supremacy of the Roman church. They also addressed the topics of repentance, free will, good works, purgatory, and indulgences although more briefly. Eck and Karlstadt then concluded the debate by continuing to explore the themes of grace, free will, and good works.

Luther's Letter to Spalatin

Luther described the course of the debate in a letter that is dated July 20, 1519 and was addressed to Georg Spalatin (1481–1545), court chaplain, secretary, and advisor of Elector Frederick of Saxony. The following is an excerpt from this letter.

> The next week Eck debated with me, at first very acrimoniously, concerning the primacy of the pope. His proof rested on

---

Carlstadt, we, George, Duke of Saxony, grant to him and to those whom he may bring with him, for the debate to take place in Leipzig with Dr. Eck, as long as he may be with us and until he returns to his own home, free and safe conduct." See Dau, 81.

16. Martin Brecht, *Martin Luther. His Road to Reformation*, trans. James L. Schaaf (Philadelphia: Fortress, 1985), 312, 316. Hereafter referred to as Brecht; Dau, 120, 193. Lyndal Roper, *Martin Luther Renegade and Prophet* (London: Vintage [Penguin Random House], 2016), 132, gives the dates June 27–July 15 for the debate.

17. Dau, 185. Martin Brecht apparently does not consider the short encounter between Eck and Luther in the early morning of July 14 to be part of the debate and thus claims that the debate between the two main antagonists ended on July 13. See Brecht, 316.

the words 'You are Peter . . .' [Matt. 16:18], and 'Feed my sheep,
. . . follow me' [John 21:17, 22], and 'strengthen your brethren'
[Luke 22:32], adding to these passages many quotations from the
church fathers. What I answered you will soon see. Then, coming to the last points, he rested his case entirely on the Council
of Constance which had condemned Huss's article alleging that
papal authority derived from the emperor instead of from God.
Then Eck stamped about with much ado as though he were in
an arena, holding up the Bohemians before me and publicly ac-
cusing me of the heresy and support of the Bohemian heretics,
for he is a sophist, no less impudent than rash. These accusations
tickled the Leipzig audience more than the debate itself.

In rebuttal I brought up the Greek Christians during the
past thousand years, and also the ancient church fathers, who
had not been under the authority of the Roman pontiff, although
I did not deny the primacy of honor due the pope. Finally we
also debated the authority of a council. I publicly acknowledged
that some articles had been wrongly condemned [by the Council of Constance], articles which had been taught in plain and
clear words by Paul, Augustine, and even Christ himself. At this
point the adder swelled up, exaggerated my crime, and nearly
went insane in his adulation of the Leipzig audience. Then I
proved by the words of the council itself that not all the articles
which it condemned were actually heretical and erroneous. So
Eck's proofs had accomplished nothing. There the matter rested.

The third week I debated penance, purgatory, indulgences,
and the power of a priest to grant absolution, for Eck did not
like to debate with Karlstadt and asked me to debate alone with
him. The debate over indulgences fell completely flat, for Eck
agreed with me in nearly all respects and his former defense of
indulgences came to appear like mockery and derision, whereas
I had hoped that this would be the main topic of the debate. He
finally acknowledged his position in public sermons so that[18]
even the common people could see that he was not concerned
with indulgences. He also is supposed to have said that if I had
not questioned the power of the pope, he would readily have
agreed with me in all matters . . . Thus he does not seem to consider it wrong to affirm and deny the same thing at different
times. The people of Leipzig do not see this, so great is their stu-
pidity. Much more fantastic was the following: He conceded one
thing in the disputation hall but taught the people the opposite
in the church. When confronted by Karlstadt with the reason

18. LW 31:322 reads "than," which is clearly an error.

for his changeableness, the man answered without blinking an eye that it was not necessary to teach the people that which was debatable . . .

Meanwhile Eck is pleased with himself, celebrates his victory, and rules the roost; but he will do so only until we have published our side of the debate. Because the debate turned out badly, I shall republish my *Explanations Concerning the Value of Indulgences.*[19]

COMMENTARY

While Luther's report to Spalatin indicates that he did not view his opponent or the nature of his encounter with Eck in a favorable light, the Leipzig Debate was an important episode in the early history of the Lutheran reform movement. It certainly sharpened the conflict between the Reformer and Rome, and it confirmed Luther's emerging theological perspectives.

After Leipzig, Johannes Eck proved to be one of the most persistent and capable opponents of Luther, and he contributed significantly to that conflict. Eck was convinced that he had accomplished much during the debate and viewed himself as the obvious victor, particularly since he had demonstrated to his own satisfaction and the satisfaction of the defenders of Rome that Luther was a heretic. He had done so by goading Luther into defending teachings of Jan Hus that had been condemned at the Council of Constance, by causing the Wittenberg reformer to insist that the Council had erred, and by provoking him to challenge the universal authority of the papacy. The charge of heresy against Luther thus gained momentum after Leipzig. Eck traveled to Rome where he promoted this charge and was appointed to a commission that was to review Pope Leo X's bull *Exsurge Domine* of 1520 before it was announced publicly. The Vatican also assigned Eck and the papal nuncio, Jerome Aleander (1481–1542), the task of distributing the papal bull throughout Germany.[20] It was Eck who a decade later prepared the *Four Hundred and Four Articles,*[21] an extensive list of theological positions of the Lutheran reformers that he deemed to be heretical. This list confronted the Lutheran representatives at the Diet of

19. LW 31:320–23. See the original Latin letter in WA Br 1:420–31.

20. Brecht, 390, 395. See also Carter Lindberg, *The European Reformations,* 2nd ed. (Chichester, UK: Wiley-Blackwell, 2010), 83.

21. Robert Kolb and James A. Nestingen, eds. *Sources and Contexts of the Book of Concord* (Minneapolis: Fortress, 2001), 31–82. Hereafter referred to as Kolb and Nestingen, *Sources.*

Augsburg in 1530. In response, the Lutherans decided to present a common confession and defense of their faith and charged Philip Melanchthon (1491–1560) with the task of preparing the *Augsburg Confession.*[22] Eck was also a chief author of the *Confutation of the Augsburg Confession,*[23] which was the Roman response to the *Augsburg Confession.* After Augsburg, the Ingolstadt professor continued to defend the Roman church's theology and practices and to reiterate and explicate the charge of heresy against Luther and his supporters in numerous writings.

The Leipzig Debate also helped shape Luther's identity as an evangelical theologian and contributed to the clarification of his reforming agenda. The debate highlighted theological themes, including nature and grace, the freedom or bondage of the will, the motivation for and purpose of good works, the office of the keys, the priestly vocation, and ecclesiology, all topics of debate that remained crucial during the first three decades of the sixteenth-century Reformation. All had clear implications for Luther's ultimate priority, namely, the faithful proclamation of the gospel.

The chief focus of Luther's debate with Eck was, of course, papal power. That topic had diverse implications, especially for ecclesiology and for the question of authority within the church. With regard to the latter, it raised particular questions regarding the teaching office of the church, as that office was embodied in the papacy, and regarding the role and significance of scripture in the life of the church. Luther had not given extensive attention to the important topic of papal authority before the Leipzig Debate, although his critique of indulgences and of the whole penitential system in the 95 *Theses* was a clear, albeit indirect, challenge of papal power. However, his continuing scriptural studies and his intentional exploration of church history in preparation for the Leipzig Debate convinced Luther that claims of papal supremacy could not be supported, either on the basis of scripture or in light of the church's history. Those studies also clarified for him that both popes and councils can err and have erred. It therefore became apparent to him that papal pronouncements and conciliar decrees must be evaluated in light of scripture, which was the trustworthy and ultimate authority in matters of faith and practice. As he came to this conclusion, Luther also began to question the teaching authority of the church. While this teaching authority is important since the church is called to interpret scripture and to proclaim and teach God's word persistently and faithfully, the tradition, which is the product of this proclamation and teaching, has proven to be fallible since popes, councils, and theologians have erred at times. Tradition

22. BC 27–105.

23. Kolb and Nestingen, *Sources,* 105–39.

and, hence, the teaching office of the church, therefore cannot transcend scripture in authority. Rather, the tradition must always be evaluated in light of scripture, particularly in light of the gospel, in order to ascertain whether the church has exercised its teaching authority in a defensible manner and has interpreted scripture faithfully. Scripture thus always has authority over the church, rather than the church including the pope having authority over scripture. The Holy Spirit is the ultimate teacher of the church, and the Spirit enlivens and instructs the community of faith by means of the word of God.

Luther's study of the Bible and of church history also convinced him that the claim of papal supremacy on the part of the Western church was indefensible. While he did not call for the elimination of the papal office since he was certain that it would not exist if that was not God's will, he also insisted that the papacy is a human creation and not a divinely instituted office in the church. He was willing to grant the pope supremacy of honor, but he refused to grant the papacy supreme authority. Supremacy within the Roman church belongs to scripture and ultimately to Christ. Luther was, therefore, also inspired to articulate an ecclesiology informed by his baptismal theology, the notion of the priesthood of the baptized, an emphasis on the centrality of word and sacrament, and a gospel-centered perspective. While Luther fully recognized that some of his theological claims and his curbing of papal authority rejected specific teachings and practices of the Roman church and while he was repeatedly confronted with the charge of heresy, he was determined to interpret scripture in light of the gospel and to proclaim Christ faithfully, and to challenge the teachings, piety, and authorities of the church whenever they did not witness to Christ and thus contradicted the gospel. The Leipzig Debate strengthened Luther's determination to pursue this evangelical reforming vocation.

5

Treatise on Good Works (1520)

ANNA MARIE JOHNSON

Luther wrote the *Treatise on Good Works* against the backdrop of mounting conflict. By the spring of 1520, the ecclesial case against Luther was gaining momentum. In January of that year his case was reopened in Rome, and in February the pope established a commission to denounce Luther formally. By March, Luther had received a condemnation of certain teachings from the theological faculties of Louvain and Cologne. On June 15, 1520, the pope finally issued his bull against Luther, threatening excommunication if he did not recant.

While his case developed in Rome, Luther kept busy with his normal teaching and preaching responsibilities. In addition, his newfound fame meant that he kept up a steady correspondence with both supporters and detractors. He also continued to publish treatises on topics related to the controversy and his theology. Many of these treatises were in German, which engaged a broad audience with Luther's thought. The *Treatise on Good Works* was one of these German-language treatises.

The idea for the treatise seems to have originated in conversation with Georg Spalatin, the chancellor for Prince Frederick of Saxony. In February of 1520, Spalatin wrote Luther, reminding him of his promise to write a piece on good works.[1] By March, Luther reported to Spalatin that the treatise

---

1. WA 6:196.

was growing into a small book.[2] It was printed by early June of 1520 and reprinted eight times in that same year. The treatise was also translated into at least four other languages. It preceded Luther's better-known "Reformation Treatises" *(Address to the Christian Nobility, Babylonian Captivity of the Church,* and *The Freedom of a Christian)* by less than a month, is of similar size, and also contains major programmatic statements about his reform. By any criteria, the *Treatise on Good Works* deserves to be included in the list of major Reformation treatises. In fact, Luther scholar Scott Hendrix claims that the *Treatise on Good Works* "remains the clearest and most accessible introduction to Luther's reforming work and the theology behind it."[3]

It seems that Spalatin's and Luther's immediate motivation for this treatise was to clear up confusion about the role of good works in Christian life. When Luther argued that Christians were saved by faith, not by works, many people took this to mean that Christians were freed from good works entirely. This misunderstanding was of particular concern for rulers, who feared their constituents might interpret Luther's message as a license for lawlessness. In the *Treatise on Good Works,* Luther corrected this impression by clarifying his criticism of traditional religious works and by showing how good works proceed from faith. The treatise is structured as a commentary on the Ten Commandments in order to emphasize that Christians should follow God's commandments, not the rules and practices invented by the church.

TREATISE ON GOOD WORKS

It should be known, first of all, that no good works exist other than those that God has commanded, just as there is no sin other than what God has forbidden. Whoever wishes to identify and perform good works needs only to learn God's commandments. Accordingly, Christ says: "If you want to be saved, then keep the commandments" [Matt. 19:17]. And when the young man asks what he has to do to be saved, Christ holds up to him the Ten Commandments and nothing else [Matt. 19:11–19]. Our knowledge of good works must derive from God's commandments and not from the appearance, magnitude, or quantity of the deeds themselves, nor from human opinion, laws, or dealings. We have seen that before, and it still happens owing to our blindness and disdain for God's commandments.

---

2. WA 2:75.

3. Scott Hendrix, Introduction to *Treatise on Good Works: Luther Study Edition* (Minneapolis: Fortress, 2012), 3.

The First Good Work: "You shall have no other gods before me"[4]

The foremost and noblest good work is faith in Christ, just as he himself said when the Jews asked him what they should do in order to perform good works of God. He answered: "This is the (good) work of God, that you believe in him whom God has sent" [John 6:21–29]. Now when we hear this or preach it, we pass right over it, thinking it is a small thing that is easy to do. We should, however, pause there a long time and ponder it in depth. For all good works have to be included in this one and receive their goodness from it, as if receiving a fief. We have to make it simple and clear so that it can be understood . . .[5]

This is the work of the first commandment: "You shall not have other gods." That is to say: Since I alone am God, all your confidence, trust, and faith should be placed only in me and no one else. You do not "have a god" when all you do is mouth the words or worship by bowing the knee or making external gestures instead of trusting God from the heart and counting on God's goodness, grace, and favor in all that you do or suffer, in living and dying, in weal and in woe, just as Christ said to the Samaritan woman: "I say to you, whoever worships God must worship in spirit and truth" [John 4:24]. And this faith, trust, and confidence, which come from the bottom of the heart, are the true fulfillment of the first commandment. Without them no work of any kind can satisfy its demand . . .[6]

. . . Note the gap between fulfilling the first commandment only with external works and fulfilling it with innermost trust. The latter makes genuine and lively children of God, while the former produces a ruinous idolatry and the most harmful hypocrites on earth. With their pretentious displays, they lead countless people astray, keep them from faith, and leave them woefully seduced, in external mirages and specters . . .[7]

The Second Good Work: "You shall not make wrongful use of the name of the LORD your God"[8]

The first commandment forbids us to have other gods. As a consequence, it commands us to have the one true God by means of firm faith, trust,

---

4. The heading and the wording of the first commandment are absent in Luther's text.

5. AL 267–68.

6. AL 1:274–75.

7. AL 1:278.

8. The text of the commandment is absent in Luther's version.

confidence, hope, and love. With those works alone can we possess, honor, and hold fast to the one God. No other work enables us to draw close to God or depart from God. This happens through faith or unbelief, through trust or doubt. No other work ever reaches up to God. In the same way, the second commandment prohibits us from taking God's name in vain. But that is not all. It also commands us to honor, invoke, praise, proclaim, and exalt his name. That is to say, it is not possible to avoid dishonoring God's name when it is not properly honored. For although it may be honored with the mouth, genuflections, kisses, or other actions, when they do not proceed from the heart through faith, trusting God's favor, the result is nothing but pretense and a hypocritical appearance.

See how many good works a person can do all day long in this commandment and never be without the good works of this commandment, even if undertaking no more pilgrimages or visits to shrines. So tell me, does a moment ever pass in which we do not continuously receive God's blessings or suffer evil misfortune? What are these things but constant admonitions and encouragements to praise, honor, and bless God and to call upon him and his name? Even if you did nothing in other matters, would you not have enough to do with this commandment alone by blessing, singing to, praising, and honoring God's name unceasingly? . . .[9]

From this arises the astonishing but just judgment of God, that sometimes a poor person, whom no one can imagine doing many and great works, when at home alone praises God joyfully when things are going well or calls upon God with complete confidence when something bad happens. In so doing that individual performs a greater, more God-pleasing work than another person who frequently fasts, prays, endows churches, makes pilgrimages, and is busy doing great deeds everywhere. Such a fool gawks and looks for even greater works to the point of being so completely blinded as to miss the greatest work of all. In the eyes of such fools, praising God is a very small thing in contrast to the fabulous image of these self-invented works, in which such individuals presumably praise themselves more than God or which please them more than God does. With their good works they rage against the second commandment and its works . . .[10]

9. AL 1:287.
10. AL 1:288.

The Third Commandment: "Remember the Sabbath day and keep it holy"[11]

The first work of this commandment, which we commonly call worship, is unsophisticated and easily grasped: attending Mass, praying, and listening to the sermon on Sundays and holy days. According to this definition, this commandment entails only a few works. If, however, they are not done with faith and trust in God's goodwill, they are nothing, as we said earlier . . .

At the Mass, it is necessary that we be present with our heart as well; this happens when we practice faith in our hearts. We have to repeat the words that Christ spoke when he instituted the Mass: "'Take and eat; this is my body given for you.' In the same manner, he took the cup and said: 'Take and drink from it, all of you; that is the new, eternal covenant in my blood, which is poured out for you and for many for the forgiveness of sins. As often as you drink it, do it in remembrance of me'" [Matt 26:21–28 and 1 Cor. 11:21–25]. With these words, Christ established for himself a memorial or anniversary Mass to be celebrated for him daily throughout Christendom. And he attached to it a glorious, rich, and generous will and testament, which grants and establishes for us not annuities, money or worldly possessions but the forgiveness of all our sins, grace, and mercy unto eternal life so that everyone who comes to this memorial shall possess this testament. Christ has died so that the testament became durable and irrevocable . . .

Wherever this testament is rightly preached, however, it is necessary that we listen attentively, comprehend and retain it, continually meditate on it, and thereby strengthen faith against all attacks of sin—past, present, or future . . .

The sermon should entice sinners to feel remorse for their sin and inflame the desire for this treasure. It follows that it must be a grave sin for those who do not listen to the gospel and who spurn this treasure and the rich meal to which they are invited. A much graver sin, however, is committed by those who do not preach the gospel and thereby allow those who would gladly have heard it go to ruin, although Christ has steadfastly commanded them to preach the gospel and this testament. In fact, he did not want the Mass to be celebrated unless the gospel was also preached . . .

People should pray, but not in the customary way by turning pages in the prayer book or counting beads on the rosary. Instead, we should bring particularly pressing needs [before God], earnestly seek aid, and place our faith and trust in God so intently that we have no doubt we will be heard . . .[12]

11. The text of the commandment is absent in Luther's version.

12. AL 1:303–6.

The spiritual meaning of this commandment contains an even greater work that encompasses human nature in its entirety. Here one has to realize that in Hebrew *sabbath* means "cease working" or "rest," because "on the seventh day God rested from all the works that he had done" [Gen. 2:2] . . .

This rest or cessation of work is twofold: bodily and spiritual; hence, the commandment must be understood in two ways. Physical refraining from work and resting were addressed earlier: we stop the works of our hands and our labor in order to assemble in church, be present at Mass, listen to God's word, and pray communally and with one accord . . .

Spiritual rest, for which above all else God intended this commandment, entails not only laying down our work and labor but—much more—letting God alone work in us without applying any power of our own at all . . .

If God is to work and live in them, all these vices and corruption must be strangled and stamped out so that a rest and ceasing of all our works, words, thoughts, and lives may take place—so that from now on, as Paul says, "not we, but Christ lives in us," acts and speaks [Gal. 2:20] . . . Here is the source of good works like fasting, keeping vigils, and performing strenuous labors . . .[13]

The First Commandment of the Second Table of Moses: The Fourth Commandment: "Honor your father and mother"[14]

From this commandment we learn that after the noble works required by the first three commandments there is no greater work for us than to obey and serve those whom God has appointed as authorities over us. For this reason, disobedience is even worse than murder, unchastity, theft, dishonesty and anything else covered by the last six commandments . . .

The first work of this commandment is to honor our biological fathers and mothers. This honor does not only consist in outward gestures but also in obedience to them, keeping their words and deeds in mind, showing them respect and treating them as important, agreeing with what they say, remaining quiet and putting up with how they treat us unless it violates the first three commandments, and providing them as needed with food, clothing, and shelter . . .[15]

Thus, it is true, as they say, that parents, if they had done nothing else, can gain salvation by means of their children. And if parents raise them for serving God, then they really have both hands full of good works for

13. AL 1:321–23.

14. "The Fourth Commandment" is absent in Luther's text.

15. AL 1:330–31.

themselves. For who are the hungry, thirsty, naked, imprisoned, sick, and strangers [Matt. 25:31–46] save the souls of your own children? With them God makes your house into a hospice with you as the administrator . . .[16]

The second work of this commandment is to honor and obey our spiritual mother, the holy Christian church, and its spiritual authorities. We should follow whatever they command, forbid, set down, order, ban, or allow. Just as we honor, fear, and love our natural parents, so also we should let the spiritual authorities be right in all matters that do not contradict the first three commandments.

This second work is almost more difficult than the first. The spiritual authorities are supposed to punish sin with the ban and other legal measures and to urge their spiritual children to be upright, so they might have cause to perform these works and exercise themselves in obedience and respect toward the authorities. One sees no such diligence now, however, and they set themselves against their subjects like the mothers who run away from their children to their lovers, as Hosea states [Hosea 2:7]. They do not preach, teach, guard against anything, or punish anybody. There is no longer any spiritual authority in Christendom . . .[17]

The third work of this commandment is to obey civil authorities, as Paul, Titus, and St. Peter teach [Rom. 13:1–7; Titus 3:1; 1 Pet. 2:11–17]. Be subject to the king as the supreme ruler and to the princes as his delegates and to all the ranks of worldly power. Its work is to protect those subject to it and to punish thievery, robbery, and adultery. . .

In all of this, we should bear in mind what St. Peter commanded us to remember: whether the authorities exercise their power justly or unjustly, it cannot hurt the soul but only the body and what we possess . . .[18]

The Fifth Commandment: "You shall not murder"[19]

. . .The following commandments take up human desires and lusting in order to slay them.

There are the angry and vengeful passions of which the fifth commandment speaks: "You shall not kill." The work of this commandment is very comprehensive, drives out vice, and is called gentleness. This gentleness is of two kinds. The first kind sparkles beautifully, but there is nothing behind it. We direct it to friends and to others who help and support us in

16. AL 1:335.

17. AL 1:337–38.

18. AL 1:342–43.

19. The text of the fifth commandment is absent from Luther's text.

matters that concern our property and reputation or who do not injure us in word or deed . . .

The other kind of gentleness is good to the core and is revealed toward adversaries and enemies. It does not hurt them, does not take revenge, does not curse, insult, or spread lies about them; does not even wish bad things on them, even though they might have taken away property, reputation, body, and friends—everything. Wherever possible, this gentleness returns good for evil, speaks well of them, wishes them the best, and prays for them . . .[20]

The Sixth Commandment: "You shall not commit adultery"

A good work is also commanded in this commandment. It includes many things, drives out many vices, and is called purity or chastity. About this much has been written and preached so that almost everyone knows about it, even if they do not take it to heart and practice is as diligently as they do the works that are not commanded. (We are quite ready to do what is not commanded and to leave undone what is commanded!) We observe that the world is full of shameful, unchaste deeds and scandalous sayings, fables, and ditties. Moreover, incentives daily pile up to indulge in gluttony, drunkenness, idleness, and excessive displays of jewelry and finery. Meanwhile, we carry on as if we were Christians when we have attended church, said our little prayers, and observed our fast and feast days, as if that were enough.

If, however, no other work than chastity were commanded, we would have our hands full obeying it alone. Unchastity is a very dangerous and rabid vice that infects all our members: the heart through our thoughts; the eyes in our looking; the ears through what we hear; the mouth in what we say; our hands, feet, and entire body with what we do. To keep it in check requires enormous work and effort . . .

The work of chastity, should it endure, results in many other good works: fasting and moderation against gluttony and drunkenness, vigils and early rising against laziness and oversleeping, labor and effort against idleness . . .

Do you see? Each and every person will be completely swamped, find enough to do for oneself and be overwhelmed in him- or herself with countless good works. At present, however, no one uses praying, fasting, alertness, and labor to ward off vice; they are considered ends in themselves even though they were instituted to accomplish the work of this commandment and to cleanse us more and more each day . . .[21]

20. AL 1:351–52.
21. AL 1:354–56.

The Seventh Commandment: "You shall not steal"

This commandment, too, includes a work that consists of many good works and opposes many vices. In German, it is called "generosity." This is a work that involves each and every individual being ready to use his or her possessions to help and serve. It fights against not only theft and robbery but any damage to worldly possessions that one person can inflict on another, for example, through greed, usury, overcharging, cheating, selling inferior goods or using false weights and measures. Who can recount all the clever new tricks that increase every day in business? Everyone searches for an advantage to the disadvantage of others; they forget the law that says, "Whatever you wish others to do to you, do also to them." [Matt. 7:12]. . .

Faith by itself teaches the work of this commandment. For if the heart anticipates God's favor and relies on it, how is it possible for faith to be greedy and full of cares? It must be certain beyond any doubt that God receives us. For this reason faith does not cling to any money at all but instead uses it with joyful generosity for the benefit of others—knowing all along that we will have enough for any needs because the God in whom it trusts will never deceive or forsake it . . .

Indeed, in this commandment one can clearly see how all good works must arise from and be done in faith. For everyone can see without a doubt that the cause of avarice is mistrust, while the cause of generosity is faith because the person who trusts God is generous and does not have doubts about not having enough at any time. And vice versa: a person is greedy and anxious because of not trusting God . . .[22]

The Eighth Commandment: "You shall not bear false witness against your neighbor"

This commandment appears trivial at first but is in fact so vast that whoever would keep it correctly must stake everything—body and life, goods and reputation, friends and all possessions—on it. And yet it involves only the work of one small bodily member: the tongue. In German, it is called speaking the truth and refuting lies wherever necessary. Thus, many of the tongue's evil works are forbidden here: both those that happen through speaking and those that occur in silence. Through speaking, for example, when someone has a fraudulent case in a court of law and tries to defend it with falsehoods or to trick one's neighbor with deceit—using anything to make one's own case look better and stronger while passing over in silence

22. AL 1:357-60.

and downplaying anything that would help the good case of the neighbor. With such behavior, however, these individuals are not treating the neighbor as they would like the neighbor to treat them. Some people act that way out of selfishness, and others do it to avoid damages or disgrace, but either way they are seeking what they want more than God's commandment . . .[23]

The Ninth and Tenth Commandments: "You shall not covet your neighbor's house; you shall not covet your neighbor's wife, or male or female slave, or ox, or donkey, or anything that belongs to your neighbor"[24]

The last two commandments, which forbid the evil bodily appetites, lust, and envy of worldly goods are clear in themselves and remain in place without harming the neighbor. Even so these things remain right up to the grave, and the internal struggle against them remains until death. For that reason, St. Paul merged these two commandments into one and set one goal for them that we do not reach but can only envision until death [Rom. 7:7]. No one has ever been so holy that no evil inclination was felt when the cause and the stimulus were right there. For original sin is by nature innate in us. It can be dampened but never rooted out except by bodily death, which for that reason is both useful and desirable. May God help us. Amen.[25]

COMMENTARY

With exhaustive detail and forceful argumentation, the *Treatise on Good Works* makes clear that following Luther would not free Christians from responsibilities towards God and others. While Luther emphasizes that only faith can fulfill the commandments, he also shows how genuine faith propels Christians to love and honor others. Luther repeatedly contrasts sincere and sacrificial works of love with the most common late medieval religious works, such as the veneration of saints, pilgrimages, endowing masses, saying set prayers, and many others. In his view, all these works are attempts to avoid following the Ten Commandments and instead to do works that are ostentatious or in the self-interest of the doer. Luther comes down particularly hard on perfunctory worship, in which people go through the motions

---

23. AL 1:361–62.

24. The heading and wording of the ninth and tenth commandments are absent in Luther's text.

25. AL 1:366–67.

of worship but without any engagement of the heart to strengthen faith. Such worship, he claims, actually makes faith weaker because it produces the illusion of faith instead of true faith.

In many instances throughout the *Treatise on Good Works,* Luther connects his explanation of the Ten Commandments with his movement. We saw this above in his discussion of the fourth commandment, in which respect for one's parents was extended to respect for the church—but only inasmuch as both parents and church support the first three commandments. Again, faith in God is the plumb line. In a similar fashion, Luther interprets the commandment against false witness as a commandment to speak the truth to church and political officials, even if it means persecution and sacrifice. Criticizing those who remain silent out of self-interest, Luther writes, ". . . they have no faith in God and expect from God nothing good for themselves. Where this confidence and faith are present, you find also a courageous, valiant, and dauntless heart that risks everything and stands by the truth come what may, even against pope and kings, as those precious martyrs once did."[26]

In many ways, the *Treatise on Good Works* is a summation of Luther's reforming career up to 1520, which focused first on indulgences and then on other ways that Luther saw the medieval church leading its sheep astray. In the *Treatise on Good Works* Luther outlined the shape of the Christian life by connecting his focus on the Bible, his emphasis on grace, his criticisms of late medieval religion, and his criticisms of the church. The other "Reformation Treatises" of 1520 continued these insights and expanded them to address further implications of Luther's discerning understanding of faith and works.

FOR FURTHER READING

Edwards, Mark U., Jr. *Printing, Propaganda, and Martin Luther.* Berkeley: University of California Press, 1994. Reprint, Minneapolis: Fortress, 2005.
Forell, George W. *Faith Active in Love: An Investigation of the Principles Underlying Luther's Social Ethics.* Minneapolis: Augsburg, 1964.
Hendrix, Scott H. *Martin Luther: Visionary Reformer.* New Haven: Yale University Press, 2015.

26. AL 1:364.

6

To the Christian Nobility (1520)

KURT K. HENDEL

THE YEAR 1520 WAS pivotal for the emerging Lutheran reform movement. By this time it was absolutely clear that the leadership of the Roman Church intended to discipline Luther, with the goal of silencing him and curbing the challenge of the church's theology and practices that he had initiated with the 95 Theses.[1] Disciplinary procedures had begun shortly after the dissemination of the 95 Theses. They continued with greater urgency after Luther's meeting with Cardinal Tomas de Vio (Cajetan) (1461–1534) from October 11–14, 1518 in Augsburg and particularly after the Leipzig Debate.[2] Luther refused to recant what he had written and taught, as Cardinal Cajetan demanded. Thus, from the perspective of Rome, Luther was unwilling to submit to the authority of the church. Furthermore, his heresy was confirmed when, in response to Johannes Eck's accusations in Leipzig, Luther admitted that some of his theological positions were similar to those of the Bohemian Reformer and condemned heretic Jan Hus (c.1361–1415). All further negotiations between Luther and Rome failed to result in the Reformer's submission to

---

1. LW 31:16–33.

2. The Leipzig Debate occurred in Leipzig from June 27–July 16, 1519. The initial debaters were Johannes Eck (1486–1543), one of the leading defenders of Rome, and Andreas Bodenstein von Karlstadt (1486–1541), one of Luther's colleagues in Wittenberg. Luther joined the debate on July 4. See Kurt K. Hendel, "Another Quincentennial: The 1519 Leipzig Debate," *Lutheran Quarterly* 32 (2018): 446–54, for a discussion of the Leipzig Debate.

Rome. Pope Leo X (1471–1521) therefore issued the bull *Exsurge Domine* on June 15, 1520. The bull threatened Luther with excommunication unless he recanted his errors within sixty days. Some of the errors were noted in the bull. Luther responded by burning the bull on December 10, sixty days after he had received it, together with a copy of canon law. Pope Leo consequently issued the bull *Decet Romanum pontificem* on January 3, 1521, thereby declaring Luther to be a heretic and excommunicating him. All those who continued to support and protect Luther were also placed under papal condemnation. Luther's future and the future of the reform movement that he had inspired were, therefore, uncertain in 1520.

Yet, Luther continued to gain support among the general populace and from fellow theologians and political leaders in spite of the ecclesiastical legal proceedings against him. The knights Ulrich von Hutten (1481–1523), Franz von Sickingen (1481–1523), and Sylvester von Schaumburg (c.1461–1534) sided with Luther and pledged to defend him, if necessary. His prince, Elector Frederick III (1461–1525), who was commonly known as Frederick the Wise, continued to protect Luther, both because his supposed heresy had not been proven and because he was enhancing the reputation of the Elector's university. Luther also continued his labors with much vigor, particularly his production of writings that promoted his reforming agenda. After the Leipzig Debate, the Reformer published sixteen treatises in the remaining months of 1519.[3] This literary productivity was quite remarkable, especially when one considers that the ecclesiastical disciplinary procedures, his extensive correspondence, his monastic duties, his continuing teaching responsibilities, and his regular preaching also required the Reformer's attention. Luther continued to publish regularly in 1520 as well, and five treatises, in particular, made significant contributions to the theological and practical reform of church and society. They were his *On the Papacy of Rome,*[4] *A Treatise on Good Works,*[5] *To the Christian Nobility of the German Nation Concerning the Improvement of the Christian Estate,*[6] *The Babylonian Captivity of the Church,*[7] and *The Freedom of a Christian.*[8]

To the Christian Nobility, which was the third of these 1520 treatises, is a programmatic statement of reform that is intentionally addressed to the political leaders of the German territories, with the encouragement that

3. LW 44:117.

4. LW 39:49–104.

5. See AL 257–367. See also LW 44:15–114.

6. AL 1:368–465. See also LW 44:115–217.

7. AL 3:8–129. See also LW 36:3–126.

8. AL 1:466–538. See also LW 31:327–77.

they foster the renewal of church and society. The treatise consists of three sections. The first is a theological exploration and explication of Luther's notions of the universal priesthood, of good order in the church, and of the doctrine of vocation. The second section focuses on three ecclesiastical abuses that should be remedied by a council, namely, the avarice of the papacy; the continuing proliferation of cardinals, which was inspired by this avarice; and the expansion of the curia, which also drained Germany's fiscal resources. The third section is a list of twenty-seven reform proposals that address problems in both church and society. This list is reminiscent of the *Gravamina* that were regularly presented to Diets of the Holy Roman Empire during the late Middle Ages. The most recent presentation of such grievances had occurred at the Diet of Augsburg in 1518.[9]

Luther completed *To the Christian Nobility* by June 23, when he sent the manuscript of the treatise to Nicholas von Amsdorf (1481-1565). The accompanying letter became the preface of the printed treatise,[10] the first edition of which was published by the Wittenberg printer Melchior Lotther (c. 1491-1542) in August 1520.[11] It consisted of four thousand copies, but Luther was preparing a slightly expanded second edition within a week of its initial publication.[12]

Various factors inspired Luther to write the treatise. He was eager to articulate his own theological perspectives and to clarify their implications for the reform of church and society. His disappointment that the papacy and the curia resisted such reforming efforts and his doctrine of the universal priesthood inclined him to turn to the political leaders for support. Thus, he already expressed the hope in his *On the Papacy of Rome*[13] and in his *A Treatise on Good Works*[14] that the political leaders would address the abuses promoted by the church. The ardent defense of papal authority by Augustine von Alveld in his *On the Apostolic See* and by Sylvester Prierias in his *Epitome of a Reply to Martin Luther* was also a factor that inspired Luther to write to Georg Spalatin (1481-1545), a secretary and advisor to Elector

9. AL 1:371.

10. AL 1:370.

11. The editors of the Weimar Ausgabe indicate that the first edition was published in the middle of August 1520. See WA 6:392. See also AL 1:370.

12. See LW 44:119. It also notes that the first edition appeared on August 18, 1520. Luther likely prepared the second edition so quickly because the four thousand copies of the first edition were sold within two weeks. See Martin Brecht, *Martin Luther. His Road to Reformation 1483-1521*, tr. by James L. Schaaf (Philadelphia: Fortress, 1985), 376.

13. LW 39:102-3.

14. AL 1:341, 346. See also LW 44:90-91, 96.

Frederick, "I have a mind to issue a broadside to Charles and the nobility of Germany against the tyranny and baseness of the Roman curia."[15] Luther fulfilled this intention with *To the Christian Nobility*.

THE TREATISE

The first section of *To the Christian Nobility* is the most noteworthy part of this work and continues to have relevance for the church's life in the twenty-first century. In it Luther clarifies the theological bases for his invitation to the political leaders to foster the reform of church and society. The ecclesiological implications of this part of the treatise are particularly significant. Luther writes:

> The Romanists have very cleverly built three walls around themselves. Hitherto they have protected themselves by these walls in such a way that no one has been able to reform them. As a result, the whole of Christendom has fallen horribly.
>
> In the first place, when secular authority has been used against them, they have made decrees and declared that secular authority has no jurisdiction over them, but that, on the contrary, spiritual authority is above secular authority. In the second place, when the attempt is made to reprove them with the Scriptures, they raise the objection that only the pope may interpret the Scriptures. In the third place, if threatened with a council, their story is that no one may summon a council but the pope . . .
>
> Let us begin by attacking the first wall. It is pure invention that pope, bishop, priests, and monks are called the spiritual estate while princes, lords, artisans, and farmers are called the secular estate. This is indeed a piece of deceit and hypocrisy. Yet no one need be intimidated by it, and for this reason: all Christians are truly of spiritual status, and there is no difference among them except that of office. Paul says in 1 Cor. 12[:11–13] that we are all one body, yet every member has its own work by which it serves the others. This is because we all have one baptism, one gospel, one faith, and all are Christians alike; for baptism, gospel, and faith alone make us spiritual and a Christian people . . .
>
> Since those who exercise secular authority have been baptized with the same baptism, and have the same faith and the same gospel as the rest of us, we must admit that they are priests

15. WA Br 2:119–20. The letter may have been written on June 7, 1520.

and bishops, and we must regard their office as one that has a proper place in the Christian community and is useful to it. For whoever has crawled out of baptism can boast that he is already a consecrated priest, bishop, and pope, even though it is not seemly that just anybody should exercise such an office. Because we are all priests of equal standing, no one must push himself forward and take it upon himself, without our consent and election, to do that for which we all have equal authority. For no one dare take upon himself what is common to all without the authority and consent of the community...Therefore, a priest in Christendom is nothing else but an officeholder...

It follows from this that there is no true, basic difference between laymen and priests, princes and bishops, or (as they say) between spiritual and secular, except that of office and work, and not that of status . . . Now consider how Christian the decree is which says that the secular power is not above the "spiritual estate" and has no right to punish it . . . I say therefore that since secular authority is ordained of God to punish the wicked and protect the good, it shoulda be left free to perform its office in the whole body of Christendom without restriction and without respect to persons, whether it affects pope, bishops, priests, monks, nuns, or anyone else . . . So I think this first paper wall is overthrown . . .

The second wall is still more loosely built and less substantial. [The Romanists] want to be the only masters of Holy Scripture, although they never learn a thing from the Bible all their life long. They assume the sole authority for themselves, and, quite unashamed, they play about with words before our very eyes, trying to persuade us that the pope cannot err in matters of faith, regardless whether he is righteous or wicked . . .

Therefore, their claim that only the pope may interpret Scripture is an outrageous fancied fable. They cannot produce a single letter [of Scripture] to maintain that the interpretation of Scripture or the confirmation of its interpretation belongs to the pope alone. They themselves have usurped this power. And although they allege that this power was given to St. Peter when the keys were given to him, it is clear enough that they keys were not given to Peter alone but to the whole community. Further, the keys were not ordained for doctrine or government, but only for the biding or loosing of sin . . .

Besides, if we are all priests, as we said above, and all have one faith, one gospel, one sacrament, why should we not also have the power to test and judge what is right or wrong in matters of faith? . . . Therefore, it is the duty of every Christian to espouse the cause of the faith, to understand and defend it, and to denounce every error.

The third wall falls of itself once the first two are down. For when the pope acts contrary to the Scriptures, it is our duty to stand by the Scriptures, to reprove him, and to constrain him,
. . .

[The Romanists] have no basis in Scripture for their claim that the pope alone has the right to call or confirm a council . . . Thus we read in Acts 15 that it was not St. Peter who called the Apostolic Council but the apostles and elders. If then that right had belonged to St. Peter alone, the council would not have been a Christian council, but a heretical *conciliabulum*. Even the Council of Nicea, the most famous of all councils, was neither called nor confirmed by the bishop of Rome, but by the emperor Constantine. Many other emperors after him have done the same, and yet these councils were the most Christian of all. But if the pope alone has the right to convene councils, then these councils would all have been heretical. Further, when I examine the councils the pope did summon, I find that they did nothing of special importance.

Therefore, when necessity demands it, and the pope is an offense to Christendom, the first one who is able should, as true members[16] of the whole body, do what can be done to bring about a truly free council. No one can do this so well as the secular authorities, especially since they are also fellow-Christians, fellow-priests, fellow-participants in spiritual authority, sharing power over all things. Whenever it is necessary or profitable, they ought to exercise the office and work that they have received from God over everyone.[17]

COMMENTARY

Luther's 1520 treatises clarified the agenda of the reformation movement and gave a significant impetus to that movement. While Luther addressed particularly the divine-human relationship and ecclesiastical matters in the other 1520 treatises, his focus was a broader one in *To the Christian Nobility*. In this work Luther explored crucial theological themes; highlighted

16. The translation should read "as a true member" for grammatical reasons. See also LW 44:137 and WA 6:413.

17. AL 1:380–90.

ecclesiastical abuses that required attention and reform; and identified societal problems, while also suggesting effective solutions.

The thirty reforms that Luther proposed in the treatise obviously address his particular contemporary context. They are, therefore, primarily
relevant to that context and serve as historical resources for understanding
the challenges that church and society faced in Luther's time. However, the
reform proposals can also serve as a powerful reminder to the church in
the twenty-first century that it must remain cognizant of its failures, of its
need to be an *ecclesia semper reformanda*, and of its calling to be an agent
of transformation in the world. Luther can, therefore, still serve as a model
for faithful and prophetic voices in the community of faith who are inspired
by the gospel to call the church to be the Holy Spirit's means of self-renewal
and of reform in the public sphere.

The theological insights that Luther shares in the first section of *To
the Christian Nobility* were arguably the most important and transformative
contribution of the treatise in the sixteenth century. Their contemporary
relevance is also readily apparent. In this part of the treatise the Reformer
identifies and examines "three walls" that served as protection for the pope
and the curia and enabled the ecclesiastical leaders to dominate as well as
corrupt church and society. The three walls are the papal claims that political
leaders have no authority over the church and its leadership, that the pope
is the sole interpreter of Scripture, and that only the pope can call a council.

As he addresses the three walls, Luther articulates his understanding
of the universal priesthood or the priesthood of all the baptized. He insists
that baptism, not ordination, transforms the essence of the human being.
Through this sacramental rite and the related gifts of faith and of Christ's
righteousness, human beings are made priests. All Christians therefore have
the same spiritual status, whether they are ordained or not. What differ-
entiates them is the work that each is called to do. While their priesthood
constitutes their status (*Stand*), they do not all have the same office (*Amt*).

As priests, all believers have the power of word and sacrament. Luther
insists, however, that what belongs to all cannot be usurped by any. Thereby
Luther introduces the historically important Lutheran notion of "good order" and maintains that the community of faith must publicly choose some
of its members who are given the vocation of proclaiming God's word and
administering the sacraments within the community. These are the people
who are called to the pastoral office.

Luther emphasizes further that the diverse vocations of Christians are
spiritual callings because spiritual people pursue them. Thus, every vocation, not only the pastoral calling, is an opportunity presented by God to
serve God and the neighbor. In light of this assertion, Luther also briefly

mentions the two governances theory in the treatise. Spiritual authority and temporal authority are both God's creation, and those who exercise either of these callings make crucial contributions to the communal life of human beings. Luther's doctrine of vocation thus assures people of faith that they can be engaged in the faithful service of God in the diverse vocations that they pursue and through which they benefit their fellow human beings.

Like his notion of the priesthood of the baptized, Luther's vocational theology was a radical reorientation of the medieval world view that divided people into the "spiritual estate," which consisted of the ordained, and the "temporal estate," which consisted of the lay members of church and society. This distinction insisted that only the members of the "spiritual estate" pursued a spiritual vocation that focused on the service of God. This vocation was, therefore, more pleasing to God and, ultimately, more meritorious than any of the vocations of the laity. Luther's theology rejected this medieval worldview, elevated the laity to a position of spiritual equality with the clergy, and affirmed all faithful vocations as opportunities to serve God and the neighbor. It, therefore, presented a radical challenge to the clerical hierarchy and offered powerful good news to all who were not ordained. It is not surprising that some of the latter, particularly those who constituted the peasant class in medieval society, began to draw implications from this new theological perspective for their social, economic, and political status. The 1525 Peasants' War is indicative of this development.

It can, therefore, be asserted that the theology Luther explicated in *To the Christian Nobility* had a democratizing effect, not only within the church but in traditional societal structures as well. Luther's theology thus provided the basis for the dismantling of the medieval view of the divine–human relationship as well as of human relationships. Luther's goal in the treatise was to re-envision the spiritual nature of Christian believers and to stress the spiritual equality of all the baptized in God's eyes. As he did so, the Reformer did not intend to precipitate radical social change. Nevertheless, he certainly prepared the way for the possibility of such change.

Luther's defense of the priesthood of the baptized, his vision of vocation, and his notion of good order were creative resources for the reform of church and society in his own time. They can still play this crucial role in shaping ecclesiastical and societal ideals and structures in the twenty-first century. *To the Christian Nobility* is well worth commemorating, five hundred years after its publication.

7

On the Babylonian Captivity of the Church (1520)

ERIK HERRMANN

"By the waters of Babylon we sit down and weep, when we remember thee, O Zion. On the willows there we hang up our lyres" (Ps. 137:1). Overcome with grief, Israel could not sing for their captors. They were at a loss for words. Apparently this was not a problem for Luther. Luther would sing—he would sing high and loud and the captors would know that there still was a God in Israel. "I know another little song about Rome and the Romanists. If their ears are itching to hear it, I will sing that one to them, too—and pitch it in the highest key!"

Babylon was a powerful trope. The Apocalypse made it a symbol of all the decadence and profligacy of the kingdoms of the earth, that wicked harlot of the world. In *The City of God*, Augustine had identified it with the worldliness of the city of man which was also epitomized by pagan Rome. Petrarch, disgusted by the worldliness of the papacy in Avignon and the consequent influence of the French crown on the Roman church, called to mind the ancient Chaldean captivity so that Avignon was the new "Babylon of the west," holding the rest of the church hostage to its excesses. When Martin Luther invoked the phrase in 1520, it was filled with reminiscences. Luther's title of his most important Latin treatise was the most tragic of ironies. The people of God were not merely enslaved by a foreign, pagan power. The hierarchy of the church, the very head of the church, had itself become this pagan tyrant. Such was Luther's charge and its effect was simultaneously divisive and galvanizing. Georg Spalatin was worried that Luther's tone would only exacerbate the conflict. Erasmus believed the breach was now irreparable. Bugenhagen hated the text on his first read and loved it on his second. Even King Henry VIII famously got into the fray.

Although the treatise may be Luther's proverbial "mic drop," his argument and criticisms emerge from themes and precedents in late medieval theology and life. First, there is the sacramental theology and practice shaped by the rise of scholastic theology since the twelfth century. Not only were sacraments given a distinct definition and enumeration, but the main questions on the sacraments as vehicles of grace were increasingly answered through the use of philosophical concepts, especially those of Aristotle. Luther's extended critique of this scholastic development is a central feature of his argument in this treatise.[1]

Here, however, we will touch on two other areas of the treatise's medieval context: the growing discontent over the feudal relationships that shaped papal claims to temporal as well as spiritual authority, and Luther's appeal to elements of medieval pastoral care in sacramentology. In both cases, the evolution of the *causa Lutheri* is the context in which the "irreparable breach" emerges.

THE CONTEXT OF MEDIEVAL FEUDALISM

The expansion of the church's property and wealth as it assimilated into the structure of feudal society began gradually but was punctuated by several key moments. Crucial were the Gregorian reforms.[2] The theocratic claims of nobility and monarchy along with the exercise of proprietary rights over church affairs increasingly threatened even the church's spiritual authority. Yet over against these secular abuses, Pope Gregory VII's (c. 1011–1085) claim to the papacy's universal authority was decidedly enacted by the pursuance of additional feudal relationships. Consequently, prelates and great abbots became significant land owners and as such could exercise significant temporal authority and amass wealth through its benefices by rents (or *Zinsen* in German) and tithes. The Avignon papacy was able to bring greater

1. See the edition of the Babylonian Captivity in AL 3:8–129, where the annotations and notes focus especially on the theology in the scholastic tradition that stands behind both Luther's critique and also his reshaping of sacramentology.

2. See Gerd Tellenbach, *Church, State and Christian Society at the Time of the Investiture Controversy* (Oxford: Oxford University Press, 1938).

consolidation to this web of feudal relationships, and because there was no greater prelate than the bishop of Rome, there was to be no greater ecclesiastical fiefdom than that of the papacy. While this also made the church susceptible to the power and pressure of noble laymen, papal privileges were such that the "spiritual citadel" handled and distributed its divine treasures in much the same way that secular lords maintained and administered their temporal holdings. The consequence was a perceived exchange of Christian liberty for ecclesiastical liberties.[3]

In the context of feudal society the word "liberty" (Lat. *libertas*) gained a new meaning and usage in the church. Whereas the concept of liberty in the early Christian communities were expressed in the negative—freedom *from* the bondage of sin and death—"liberty" in the feudal system was oriented toward one's subjective rights and the exercise of them over (usually) property without external coercion or limits. "Thus, granting a liberty was to grant a legal privilege. Clergy already began receiving such liberties in the age of Constantine, but as the church participated in the emerging feudal system as a landowner, the notion of 'ecclesiastical liberty' had more to do with political and economic jurisdiction than liberty in a spiritual or theological sense."[4]

Luther was clearly attuned to this irony and employs the notion of liberty repeatedly throughout the treatise. The church's captivity is the result of the pope acting like a temporal lord, indeed a tyrant, more concerned about his "ecclesiastical liberties" than true Christian freedom:

> Neither pope nor bishop nor any other person has the right to impose a single syllable of law upon Christians without their consent; if anyone does, it is done in the spirit of tyranny. Therefore the prayers, fasts, donations, and whatever else the pope ordains and demands in all of his decrees, as numerous as they are iniquitous, he demands and ordains without any right whatever; and he sins against the liberty of the church whenever he attempts any such thing. Hence it has come to pass that the churchmen of our day are such vigorous guardians of "ecclesiastical liberty"—that is, of wood and stone, of lands and rents (for to such an extent has "ecclesiastical" today come to mean the same as "spiritual"!). Yet with such verbal fictions they not only take captive the true liberty of the church; they utterly destroy it, even worse than the Turk, and in opposition to the word of

3. See Marc Bloch, "Clergy and Burgesses," in *Feudal Society* (London: Folio Society, 2012), 422–30.

4. AL 3:73, note 167. For more on "liberty" in the Middle Ages and its impact on the church, see Tellenbach, *Church, State and Christian Society,* 1–25.

the Apostle: "Do not become slaves of men" [1 Cor. 7:23]. For to be subjected to their statutes and tyrannical laws is indeed to become slaves of men.[5]

The accusation that bishops and the pope have wrongly crossed over into temporal affairs would not have been a new observation, but Luther exploits it. In the *Address to the Christian Nobility*, more than once he wondered aloud if one should actually regard the pope as a temporal lord and thus simply treat him as a hostile military power or thief:

> If we wish to fight the Turk, let us begin here, where they are worst of all. If we are right in hanging thieves and beheading robbers, why do we let Roman avarice go free? He is the worst thief and robber that has ever been or could ever come into the world, and all in the holy name of Christ and St. Peter! . . .For this reason, the Christian nobility should set itself against the pope as against a common enemy and destroyer of Christendom for the salvation of the poor souls who perish because of this tyranny.[6]

The most presumptuous (and absurd) assertion of papal temporal authority was ensconced in the infamous *Donation of Constantine*. Originating sometime in the eighth century, the document based its claims on the fifth-century *Legenda Sancti Sylvestri*, which recounts supposed interactions between the Emperor Constantine and Pope Sylvester I. Grateful for being healed of leprosy, Constantine is said to have conferred the entire western empire to the jurisdiction of the pope in perpetuity. By the eleventh century, beginning with Leo IX and his dispute with the patriarch of Constantinople, the document was regularly cited by the pope to substantiate his claims of temporal authority over against real or perceived encroachments of secular rulers and lords. In the fifteenth century, Lorenzo Valla proved that the document was a forgery, for it used Latin that was not yet in existence in the fourth century, including the telling anachronism, "fief."[7]

Avarice was not a new critique of Rome—as evinced by the ingenious twelfth-century acrostic, ROMA = *Radix Omnium Malorum Avaricia* (avarice is the root of all evil). Yet every satirical, half-hearted pejorative of the earlier centuries became white-hot condemnations during the years of the Papal Schism (1378–1417). Luther's own order of Augustinian Hermits was

5. AL 3:73.

6. AL 2:407–8.

7. For a full historical treatment of the document, see Johannes Fried, *Donation of Constantine and Constitutum Constantini: The Misinterpretation of a Fiction and Its Original Meaning* (Berlin: de Gruyter, 2007).

deeply invested in the conflict with allegiance to the Roman pope playing a major role in what Eric Leland Saak has called the "Augustinian platform" for church reform.[8] In the face of the Schism, Augustinians began lecturing on Revelation at the beginning of the fifteenth century, interpreting the times as the time of the Antichrist and the end of the world. The Augustinian Antonius Rampegolus published a preaching manual, the *Figure Bibliorum*, which cast the times as an eschatological battle against the devil who assaults the church through schism, avarice, and cupidity. The prelates of the church had succumbed to avarice and the lust for power. This was the fourth beast of Daniel in the midst of Babylon, this was the beginning of the Antichrist's reign.[9]

A century later, it was Johann von Staupitz who, in his early sermons, could also look at the corruption of the church, and speak of the exile in Babylon and the captivity of the devil. In his final letter to Luther, Staupitz tries to assure Luther that though he has left the Augustinian order and necessarily submitted to the pope's authority, he "in the same way even today, still hates the Babylonian Captivity."[10]

THE CONTEXT OF THE FIDES SACRAMENTI AND THE CAUSA LUTHERI

By the summer of 1520, Luther's formal case had come to a boiling point. Rumors of a papal bull threatening Luther with excommunication had spread, and by June 15, Pope Leo X had officially issued *Exsurge Domine*, although it would not arrive in Wittenberg until October. The treatises written by Luther (and there were at least five to six major treatises published in 1520)[11] all reflected the desperate situation. By this time, the issue had moved well beyond the question of indulgences as such and on to the nature and extent of papal authority. Nevertheless, one theological point of the *Ninety-Five Theses* continued to be controverted. In thesis 7, Luther wrote the rather unremarkable statement: "God remits guilt to no one whom He does not, at the same time, humble in all things and bring into subjection to His vicar, the priest." But as he expands on this later in his *Explanations* (1518), the issue became much more focused on the centrality of faith:

8. Eric Leland Saak, *Highway to Heaven: The Augustianian Platform Between Reform and Reformation, 1292–1524* (Leiden: Brill, 2002).

9. Saak, 529–34; 584–617.

10. WA Br 3:264.35–36.

11. On the Papacy, On Good Works, Address to Christian Nobility, Treatise on the New Testament, Babylonian Captivity, Freedom of the Christian.

For you will have peace only as long as you believe in the word of that one who promised, "Whatever you loose, etc." [Mt. 16:18]. Christ is our peace, but only through faith. But if anyone does not believe this word, even though he be pardoned a million times by the pope himself, even though he confess before the whole world, he shall never know inner peace . . . So as a general rule we are not sure of the remission of guilt, except through the judgment of the priest, and not even through him unless you believe in Christ who has promised, 'Whatever you shall loose, etc." Moreover, as long as we are uncertain, there is no remission, since there is not yet remission for us . . . For the remission of sin and the gift of grace are not enough; one must also believe that one's sin has been remitted . . . It is not the sacrament, but faith in the sacrament, that justifies.[12]

This emphasis on the role of faith in the sacrament found some support in the writings of Augustine and Bernard, but Luther would especially appeal to the medieval axiom, "*Non sacramentum, sed fides sacramenti iustificat.*[13] It was this *fides sacramenti* that became a major point of contention when Luther met with the papal legate, Cardinal Cajetan, in the fall of 1518. Cajetan argued that an absolute certainty that one possessed grace could not be maintained, especially if the source of this certainty was something so facile and subjective as one's faith. Such a view undermined the entire sacerdotal-sacramental system, and he said (presciently) that "this is to build another church!" (*Hoc enim est novum Ecclesiam construere*). If faith justified, then the sacrament was superfluous. Indeed, the axiom *non sacramentum, sed fides sacramenti iustificat* seemed to be based on the advice of Pope Innocent III who was addressing an extreme case of pastoral care, namely that if a penitent, because of extenuating circumstances, is unable to receive the sacrament, his desire for and faith in the sacrament is enough to receive the sacrament's benefits.[14] The danger of starting with an extreme

12. LW 31:100–101, 104, 107.

13. See Augustine, *Tractates in the Gospel of John* 80.3, MPL 35, 1840: "*Accedit verbum ad elementum, et fit sacramentum, non quia fit, sed quia creditur*" (when the word is joined to the element, it becomes a sacrament, not because it becomes a sacrament, but because it is believed). And Bernard, *Sermon on the Annunciation*, 1.1, 3, MPL 183, 383–84: "You must above all believe that you cannot have forgiveness of sins except through the mercy of God. But add to this that you must believe and add this too, that your sins are forgiven by God. This is the testimony which the Holy Spirit brings forth in your heart, saying 'yours sins are forgiven.' For thus the Apostle concludes 'that a man is justified by faith' out of grace. This is what St. Paul says."

14. Aquinas makes a similar distinction, attributing benefits to the desire for the sacrament even when reception of the sacrament is impossible, *STh* III, q. 80, a. 1: ". . . the effect of the sacrament can be secured by every man if he receive it in desire,

circumstance is a neglect of the sacraments altogether. But Luther wants to do the opposite, not a neglect of the sacrament but a new orientation to it.

Cajetan did not fully understand Luther's concern (partly because what he read of Luther was not yet clear). Luther's privileging of faith was not a celebration of the subjective; rather Luther was arguing that the source of certainty lay in the word of Christ. Faith either believes Christ, or one calls him a liar. In this manner are such great things attributed to faith in the Scriptures—not the strength of faith as a virtue, but the strength and certainty of the promise to which it clings. Thus when Cajetan required Luther to renounce his view of the *fides sacramenti*, Luther saw this as denouncing Christ and his word. But in this "lay the whole summary of salvation!" The cardinal was asking him with one word—"*revoco*"—to deny that which made him a Christian.[15]

Furthermore, Luther repeatedly cited Matthew 16 as the reference point throughout his writings in 1518. The priest's absolution was to be believed because Christ had instituted the office of the keys. Faith was required for certainty because Christ had given Peter, the apostles, and their successors the authority to loose consciences that are bound by sin. Indeed, at this time Luther still believed that the Roman church, embodied in the papacy, was normative on matters of faith because Christ miraculously kept Rome in the truth.[16] But his meeting with Cajetan—the papal legate—began a process of disillusionment with the papacy that came to a conclusion in the early spring of 1520.

Shortly after his time before Cajetan, he began to wonder privately about the state of the papacy. If he was required to denounce the Gospel—that which freed his conscience and made him a Christian—in order to remain a faithful son of the church, what could this mean? In a letter to

---

though not in reality. Consequently, just as some are baptized with the Baptism of desire, through their desire of baptism, before being baptized in the Baptism of water; so likewise some eat this sacrament spiritually ere they receive it sacramentally. Now this happens in two ways. First of all, from desire of receiving the sacrament itself, and thus are said to be baptized, and to eat spiritually, and not sacramentally, they who desire to receive these sacraments since they have been instituted. Secondly, by a figure: thus the Apostle says (1 Corinthians 10:2), that the fathers of old were 'baptized in the cloud and in the sea,' and that 'they did eat . . . spiritual food, and . . . drank . . . spiritual drink.' Nevertheless, sacramental eating is not without avail, because the actual receiving of the sacrament produces more fully the effect of the sacrament than does the desire thereof, as stated above of Baptism."

15. WA Br 1:217.60–63.

16. "ad eam fidem, quad Romana ecclesia profitetur, omnium fides debut conformari . . . Nam et ego gratias ago Christo, quod hanc unam Ecclesiam in terris ita servat ingenti et quod solum posset probari fidem nostram esse veram miraculo, ut nunquam a vera fide ullo suo decreto recesserit." WA 1:662.30-34

Wenceslas Link, Luther asked—for the first time and with dread seriousness—whether the pope could be *the* Antichrist?[17] Still, in January of 1519,
Luther professed his belief in the pope's authority. Writing to Leo, he said:

> Now most blessed Father, before God and with all his creation
> as my witness, I did not, nor do I want today, in any way to
> assault or pull down with any type of deceit, the sovereignty of
> the Roman Church or that of your holiness. Wherefore I confess
> as thoroughly as possible that the sovereignty of this Church
> is above every other authority, and that nothing whatsoever in
> heaven or on earth is to be placed before it, aside from Jesus
> Christ, the one Lord of all . . . for there is one thing alone that
> I seek: that our Mother, the Roman Church, might not be pol-
> luted with the filth of a foreign avarice.[18]

But the real turning point came in February of 1520. (Here I think
Saak's interpretation of this event is quite correct).[19] Having been repeatedly accused of being a Hussite in his view of the church and its authority,
Luther finally read Jan Huss' treatise *de Ecclesia*. He was horrified. He *was*
a Hussite. So was Staupitz and all the Wittenbergers. So also is Paul and
Augustine—"Hussites to the letter!" Luther goes on in a letter to Spalatin
from February 14, 1520:

> I implore you just to look at the horrific black hole into which
> we are entering, without a Bohemian leader or teacher. I am
> too dumbfounded to even know what to think, seeing such a
> terrifying judgment of God among men that the true Gospel
> is considered worthy of being damned, having been torched so
> blatantly in public for over a hundred years, and that no one can
> admit it. It is the woe of the world![20]

What he had suspected with his encounter with Cajetan was true: the
Gospel had been denounced as a heresy by the Roman church. But the final
straw came ten days later. Writing again to Spalatin he says,

> I have in my hands from the printing house of Dominicus
> Schleupner, Lorenzo Valla's refutation of the Donation of Con-
> stantine, published by Hutten. *Good God!* You would be amazed
> how in God's judgment not only such impure, such crass and
> naked lies of such massive Roman darkness or Roman inquiry

17. WA Br 1:270.11–14, no. 121 (18 December 1518).
18. WA Br 1:292.31–293.45–49.
19. Saak, *Highway to Heaven*, 623–30.
20. WA Br 2:42.22–30.

have lasted through the ages, but also how they have prevailed and been handed down in Canon Law, one following after the other . . . *I am so overwhelmingly horrified in the very depths of my being* that I can scarcely no longer doubt that the *pope is that very Antichrist* which, as commonly known, the world has expected, since it all fits, how he lives, what he does, what he says, and what he proclaims.[21]

Naming the pope the Antichrist was nothing new. But Luther's view had moved beyond his Augustinian predecessors. It was not the pope who was Antichrist. *It was the papacy itself.* This apocalyptic view of his times was the decisive moment for Luther. At the end of his life, when his collected Latin works were published, he wrote a preface warning the readers that when they read his writings (if they read them at all) they need to read them judiciously, "be mindful of the fact that I was once a monk and most enthusiastic papist when I began that cause. I was so drunk, yes, submerged in the pope's dogmas, that I would have been ready to murder all, if I could have, or to cooperate willingly with the murderers of all who would take but a syllable from obedience to the pope . . . [even during the debate with Eck] I conceded human right to the pope, which nevertheless, unless it is founded on divine authority, is a diabolical lie."[22]

Now back to the *Babylonian Captivity.* How does this affect this work? Well first we see that the gloves have come off entirely. For Luther, the papacy is no longer a Christian institution, it is a tyrant, enslaving the church with its own laws and traditions. Having declared the gospel heresy 100 years ago, it should come as no surprise that the sacraments have become vehicles of power and subjugation. Here we find the center of Luther's critique: "the transposition of the divine generosity and promise of the sacrament into a human work, the justification of this practice by human opinion and tradition rather than the Scriptures, and the consequent enlargement of papal power and riches," these are for Luther, "the fundamental abuses of the church."[23]

Luther's *Leitmotif,* the correlation of the word of promise and faith in his sacramental theology, had been developing since at least his *Explanations* to the *Ninety-five Theses.* What has changed here is that the promise is no longer located in the priesthood or the successors of Peter. This is quite clear in his treatment of Penance. Luther notes that the promise (and faith) has been completely undermined by the papacy rather than guaranteed:

21. WA Br 2:48.20–49.29.

22. LW 34:328, 334.

23. AL 3:52, note 117.

the promise of penance . . . has been transformed into the most oppressive despotism, being used to establish a sovereignty which is more than merely temporal. Not content with these things, *this Babylon of ours has so completely extinguished faith* that it insolently *denies its necessity in this sacrament.* Indeed, with the wickedness of Antichrist it brands it as heresy for anyone to assert that faith is necessary.[24]

Luther goes on to disassociate the certainty of the promise from the ordained priesthood. First he speaks about private confession as a practice not with the priest but to "another Christian" from whom we receive "the word of comfort as if spoken by God. And if we accept this in faith, we find peace in the mercy of God speaking to us through our brother." Shortly afterwards, Luther cites Matthew 18 to emphasize that the promise is given to *all* Christians and not merely the priesthood: "it is not necessary to tell [their confession] to the church, that is, as these babblers interpret it, to the prelate or priest. On this matter we have further authority from Christ, where he says in the same chapter, "Whatever you bind on earth shall be bound in heaven, whatever you loose, etc." For this is said to each and every Christian . . . For Christ has given to every one of his believers the power to absolve even open sins."

Eventually Cajetan would understand what Luther was trying to argue and he would withdraw his demand for Luther to recant on the *fides sacramenti*, but it was too late. Luther could not believe that the power of the word of Christ could have been debated, much less censured, by the papacy. Sadly, the breach, for Luther, had become irreparable.

24. AL 3:86–87.

8

The Freedom of a Christian (1520)

MARK D. TRANVIK

CHANGING YOUR NAME IS not a casual act. Names mean something. They bear the weight of identity. A new name reflects a new reality. Something has interrupted the normal course of events, necessitating a change. Saul, blinded on the road to Damascus, becomes Paul. In the Roman Catholic tradition, when a cardinal ascends to the papal office, a new name is required. And so in our day Jorge Mario Bergoglio becomes Pope Francis, named after the famous saint who abandoned riches to serve the poor.

It was common in the sixteenth century for humanists to change their names to a Greek one in order to reflect their indebtedness to the classical heritage. So it is significant that in 1517, a German Augustinian friar named Martin Luder, changed his name to *Eleutherios* or the "liberated one." Of course, the new moniker proved unwieldy, and would not be in use for long. But a hint of the new identity is preserved in the "th" that is reflected in the change from Luder to Luther.[1]

Why the change of name? Because it echoes the core of Luther's new understanding of himself and the change needed in the church. It will also reverberate in the title of one of his most famous writings, *The Freedom of a Christian*, written in 1520. What follows is a brief outline of the historical context of the treatise followed by some selections from the work itself.

---

1. See Heinz Schilling, *Martin Luther: Rebel in an Age of Upheaval*, trans. Rona Johnston (Oxford: Oxford University Press, 2017) 139–40.

We conclude with a commentary on the nature of Luther's understanding of freedom.

Three years have passed since the publication of *The 95 Theses* in 1517. Like a slowly closing vise, Rome's patience with Luther is growing perilously thin. Discussions had taken place between the rebellious friar and Cardinal Cajetan, one of the finest minds in the church, but to no avail. A debate at Leipzig between Luther and the controversialist theologian, John Eck, made clear that the issue of indulgences was only the tip of the iceberg and that the real problem centered on the authority of the church to interpret Scripture. Papal offers trying to persuade Luther's prince, Frederick the Wise, to hand over his professor of theology proved futile. And so we come to the fateful year of 1520.

Luther's productivity in 1520 is nothing short of astounding. He authors five treatises that spell out in detail the consequences of his insistence that the Bible reveals a God who justifies the ungodly.[2] Two of them in particular would indicate the vast gulf separating him from Rome. In the *Address to the Christian Nobility* he attacks the church-state system that had undergirded civil and ecclesiastical authority for a thousand years. *The Babylonian Captivity of the Church* struck at the very structure of the church, proposing to pare the list of sacraments from seven to two. Small surprise that heresy proceedings were in the offing. An infection in the body this serious could simply not be allowed to spread. Added to all this was the election of a new and very pious emperor, Charles V, who was determined to demonstrate his zeal as a faithful son of the church.

By the autumn of 1520 it seemed inevitable that Martin Luther would soon be tried for false teaching and suffer the fate of others so accused: burning at the stake. But a papal ambassador, Karl von Miltitz, who had tried repeatedly and unsuccessfully for almost two years to mediate the dispute, makes one last ditch effort to bring the two sides together. In hindsight this appears to be a fool's errand. A papal bull threatening excommunication (*Exsurge Domini*) had been promulgated in June. This document did not mince words. The language was sharp and uncompromising, characterizing Luther as a bull loose in the vineyard of the Lord. But it was theoretically still possible for Luther to remain in the church if he repented of his false views. This would happen if he reversed himself within sixty days of the bull's publication in his region of Germany. So the door remained cracked open slightly. Miltitz met with Luther and as a result the latter agreed to

---

2. In addition to *The Freedom of a Christian*, they are, in chronological order, *Treatise on Good Works* LW 44:17–114, *The Papacy in Rome: An Answer to the Celebrated Romanist in Leipzig* (LW 39:55–104), *Address to the Christian Nobility* (LW 44:123–217) and *The Babylonian Captivity of the Church* (LW 36:11–126).

write a letter to Pope Leo X. He also would append a short writing, which became *The Freedom of a Christian.*

Given the historical situation, the sharp rhetoric of the letter strikes most readers as strange. If Luther is really serious about taking advantage of this last opportunity to be reconciled to the church, then why is this letter so harshly critical of the papal curia? One can understand his frustration with Rome's delays and fabrications but is it really possible to separate the *person* of the pope from these broadsides, as the reformer claims to be doing? There is very little evidence that Leo actually read the letter so the question is moot from one perspective. But perhaps, as Berndt Hamm has said, Luther is trying to apply the lessons of *The Freedom of the Christian* to the pope.[3] In other words, harsh language is necessary for those (the papal advisors and theologians like Eck) who suffocate Christian freedom under a blanket of rules, regulations, laws, and false views of the church. But even the enemy deserves the Christian's love and this is why Luther is generous toward the person of the pope.

The letter is a fascinating and perplexing historical document. But much more important is the short "summary of the entire Christian life" that Luther dedicated to Leo and appended to the epistle, *The Freedom of a Christian.*[4] While not entirely free of barbs, it lacks the polemics and sense of opposition that is found in many of the reformer's writings. After a brief introduction, it breaks down into two essential parts, the freedom that comes from faith in Christ and the love that flows from this liberty towards the neighbor.

THE FREEDOM OF CHRISTIAN

Many people view the Christian faith as something easy and some even place it among the virtues. They do this because they have not experienced faith nor have they tasted its great power. A person must experience the strength faith provides in the midst of trials and misfortune. Otherwise it is not possible to write well about faith or to understand what has been written about it. But one who has had even a small taste of faith can never write, speak, reflect, or hear enough concerning it. As Christ says, it is a "spring of water welling up to eternal life" (John 4.14).

---

3. Berndt Hamm, "Luther's 'Freedom of a Christian' and the Pope," *Lutheran Quarterly* 21 (2007): 249–67.

4. Martin Luther, *The Freedom of a Christian*, trans. and intro. Mark D. Tranvik (Minneapolis: Fortress, 2008), 45. Hereafter cited as *Freedom*.

Although I cannot boast of my own abundance of faith and I also know quite well how short my own supply is, nevertheless I hope I have attained at least a drop of faith—though I grant that I have been surrounded by great and various temptations. However, I hope in what follows that I am able to discuss faith in a way that is more elegant, and certainly with more clarity, than has been done in the past by the literalists and subtle disputants, who have not even understood what they have written.

In order to make the way smoother for the average or common readers (for only them do I serve) I will put forth two themes concerning the freedom and bondage of the spirit.

A Christian is lord of all, completely free of everything. A Christian is a servant, completely attentive to the needs of all.

These two assertions appear to conflict with one another. However, if they can be found to be in agreement it would serve our purposes beautifully. Both are statements from the Apostle Paul. He says in I Corinthians 9.19: "For though I am free with respect to all, I have made myself a slave to all." And in Romans 13.8 he asserts: "Owe no one anything except to love one another." It is in the very nature of love to be attentive to others and to serve the one who is loved. So it is the case with Christ. Although he was Lord of all and "born of woman, born under the law" (Galatians 4.4) he was at the same time a free man and servant, in "the form of God" and in the "form of a slave" (Philippians 2.1–7).[5]

Let us begin by looking inside ourselves at the righteous, free and true Christian, that is, the spiritual, new and inner person, and observe how the transformation to this state occurs. It is evident that nothing external can produce Christian righteousness or freedom. Nor can anything external produce unrighteousness or servitude. This can be proven by a simple argument. How is the soul able to benefit if the body is in good health—free, active, and in general, eating and drinking and doing what it pleases? Is it not the case that even the most godless slaves of wickedness can enjoy such pleasures? On the other hand, how will poor health or captivity or hunger or thirst or any other external misfortune harm the soul? Even the most godly people and those with free consciences are afflicted with such things. None of this touches upon the freedom or servitude of the soul . . .[6]

One thing and one thing alone leads to Christian life, righteousness and freedom. This is the holy Word of God, the gospel of Christ, as Jesus himself says in John 11.25: "So if the Son makes you free you will be free indeed."[7]

5. *Freedom*, 49–50.

6. *Freedom*, 51–52.

7. *Freedom*, 52.

You may ask, "What is the Word of God and how should it be used, since there are so many words of God?" I respond by quoting what Paul says in Romans 1. The Word is the gospel of God concerning his son, who was made flesh, suffered, rose from the dead, and was glorified through the Spirit who makes us holy. To preach Christ means to feed the soul, make it righteous, set it free and save it, provided the preaching is believed. For faith alone is the saving and efficacious use of the Word of God . . .[8]

You might wonder how faith alone, without the works of the law, can justify and confer so many great benefits when it appears that the Bible commands that we do a multitude of works, laws and ceremonies. Here is how I handle this question. First, it is crucial to remember what has been said above, namely, that faith alone without works of the law is what justifies, frees and saves. It should be pointed out that the entire Scripture of God is divided into two parts: commands and promises. The commands teach what is good. However, the good that is taught is not done. The commands show us what we ought to do but they do not give us the power to do it. Thus the commands function in this way: they teach us to know ourselves. By means of the commandments we recognize our inability to do the good and thereby cause us to despair of our own powers. This explains why they are called the Old Testament and belong to the old testament. For example, the commandment "You shall not covet" is a precept that proves all of us are sinners. For none of us can avoid coveting, no matter how hard we might struggle against it . . .[9]

Since these promises of God are holy, true, righteous, free and peaceful words, full of goodness, the soul which clings to them with a firm faith will find itself not only united with these promises but fully absorbed by them. It will share in the power of the promises and, even more, it will be saturated and intoxicated by them. . .[10]

The third incomparable benefit of faith is that it unites the soul with Christ just as a bride is united with her bridegroom. By this solemn promise, as the Apostle Paul teaches, Christ and the soul become one flesh. And if they are one flesh there is a true marriage between them—indeed, the most perfect of marriages because human marriages are but a shadow of this one true union. Given the marriage between Christ and the soul, it follows that they hold everything in common, the good as well as the evil. Accordingly, the soul that trusts Christ can boast and glory in him since it regards what he has as its own. And it follows that whatever the soul has Christ claims as his own.

8. *Freedom*, 53.

9. *Freedom*, 57.

10. *Freedom*, 59.

Let us look at this exchange in more detail and we shall be able to see its invaluable benefits. Christ is full of grace, life and salvation while the soul is full of sins, death and damnation. Now let faith enter the picture and sins, death and damnation are Christ's while grace, life and salvation will be the soul's. For if Christ is a bridegroom he must take upon himself that which are his bride's and he in turn bestows on her all that is his. If he gives her his body and very self, how shall he not give her all that is his? And if he takes the body of his bride, how shall he not take all that is hers?

The result is a most pleasing picture, not only of communion but of a blessed battle that leads to victory, salvation and redemption. For Christ is God and man in one person. He has not sinned or died and he is not condemned. Nor can he sin, die or be condemned. The righteousness, life and salvation he possesses are unconquerable for he is eternal and all-powerful. However, by the wedding ring of faith he shares in the sins, death and hell of his bride. In fact, he makes them his own and acts as if they were his own. It is as if he sinned, suffered, died and descended into hell in order to overcome them all. However sin, death and hell could not swallow him. In fact, they were swallowed by him in a mighty duel or battle. For his righteousness is greater than all sin, his life stronger than death, and his salvation more invincible than hell. Thus the soul that trusts Christ and receives him as its bridegroom through its pledge of faith, is free from all sins, secure against death and hell, and given eternal righteousness, life and salvation . . .[11]

Finally, we shall deal with those things that pertain to the neighbor. For we do not live in this mortal body and focus only on it. Rather, we live with all other people on earth. Indeed, we live for others and for ourselves . . .[12]

Let us be clear that no one needs to do these things to attain righteousness and salvation. Therefore we should be guided in all our works by this one thought alone—that we may serve and benefit others in everything that is done, having nothing else before our eyes except the need and advantage of the neighbor . . .[13]

From faith there flows a love and joy in the Lord. From love there proceeds a joyful, willing and free mind that serves the neighbor and takes no account of gratitude or ingratitude, praise or blame, gain or loss. We do not serve others with an eye toward making them obligated to us. Nor do we distinguish between friends and enemies or anticipate their thankfulness or ingratitude. Rather we freely and willingly spend ourselves and all that we

11. *Freedom*, 62–63.

12. *Freedom*, 79.

13. *Freedom*, 79–80.

have, whether we squander it on the ungrateful or give it to the deserving. This is just as our Father does . . .[14]

But, freely in Christ, our heavenly Father has come to our aid. So our works ought to be directed freely toward our neighbor. Each of us should become a Christ to the other. And as we are Christ to one another the result is that Christ fills us all and we become a truly Christian community.[15]

This teaching tells us that the good we have from God should flow from one to the other and be common to all. Everyone should "put on" his neighbor and act toward him or her as if we were in the neighbor's place. The good that flows from Christ flows into us. Christ has "put on" us and acted for us as if he had been what we are. The good we receive from Christ flows toward those who have need of it . . .

In conclusion, as Christians we do not live in ourselves but in Christ and the neighbor. Otherwise we are not Christian. As Christians we live in Christ through faith and in the neighbor through love. Through faith we are caught up beyond ourselves into God. Likewise, through love we descend beneath ourselves through love to serve our neighbor.[16]

COMMENTARY

I have a colleague who teaches at a prestigious university in the eastern part of the United States. It is the kind of institution that is a golden ticket to all sorts of opportunities in graduate schools and jobs. But there is also an irony because all is not well. This colleague reports that he has never seen such high levels of anxiety and concern in his classrooms. The demands of a merciless meritocracy are etched on the faces of the students. Surrounded by wealth and resources, they have absorbed the message that the promised heaven of material, social and professional success will be theirs if, and only if, they earn the requisite grades and internships and recommendations. Indeed, their very sense of identity rests on their ability to measure up to the lofty expectations set by family, culture, and ultimately, themselves.

We are separated from Martin Luther's *The Freedom of a Christian* by five hundred years. Yet, if we allow for the obvious differences, his world in some ways is not that different from our own. The revelation to him of a faith that operated outside the normal channels of human performance ("you get what you deserve") proved so liberating that he ended up shaking the theological and political foundations of sixteenth-century Europe.

14. *Freedom*, 83.
15. *Freedom*, 83–84.
16. *Freedom*, 88–89.

Within a span of three decades, almost half of the continent switches its religious allegiance. The spark for this revolution is laid out in this little treatise. And his words can still resonate today in the ears of ordinary and privileged people alike.

Luther makes clear at the outset of the treatise that the word of freedom does not operate in a vacuum. The gospel is not abstract. It always strikes listeners in the midst of their daily lives as family members, citizens and churchgoers. We must guard against the concept that we hear the Word and then we take it out into the world and "apply" it. In other words, there is no separation of being and doing, faith and ethics. Thus Luther pairs freedom and service or love in his opening paragraphs. He states that they need to fit together and not be isolated from each other. Like "saint and sinner," there is a simultaneity to faith and love. While it is true that love flows from faith and is only truly possible in faith, it is also inconceivable to Luther that the two would somehow be separated. A good tree will bear good fruit and does not need to be told to do so.

The first part of the treatise deals with the nature of freedom. Luther begins by noting that nothing "external" can make a person righteous or worthy. In his day, external works included pilgrimages, indulgences, and becoming a priest or monk. Again, the link with our time is not hard to make. We also live "outside in." We believe things external to us like wealth, respectability and degrees will somehow make for happiness and a stable identity. They will "save" us or make us whole. (It is interesting to note that one of the root meanings of the word *salvus*—the word we use for saved is "whole.") However, Luther says the path to proving our own worth leads to folly. Only one thing is truly necessary: the knowledge that we are loved and forgiven in Christ's death and resurrection.

At this point Luther has to confront a problem. If we are not saved by works, then why does the Bible have so many commands? Luther reminds his readers that God speaks with two voices in Scripture. There is the voice of the law, which makes clear how high the bar is. On a human level, external behavior is the ultimate measure. For example, no one will be sentenced to prison for *thinking* about stealing a car. But God searches the heart and the truth about us is revealed. I tell my students that a careful reading of Matthew 5–7 (the Sermon on the Mount) is not a feel-good experience. We are not inclined to turn the other cheek when struck. We have a hard time loving our enemies. The law shines a bright light into the dark corners of our lives and exposes our hypocrisy and weakness.

But there is another voice in the Bible—the one where God makes a promise. When he speaks of this promise, Luther has a hard time containing himself. It is a word of power that "saturates" and "intoxicates" the soul.

God in Christ breaks into our lives and shatters all our foolish attempts to construct a life based on reputation, respectability and wealth. A new identity is given in Christ and Luther turns to the most intimate of human relationships—marriage—to explain what he means. I do not need to repeat Luther's words here and any attempt to approximate his passion for God's love in Christ would be a poor imitation. Rather I suggest a careful reading of the section above on how Christ the bridegroom weds an wholly unworthy bride (us!) and gives to his beloved everything she lacks while taking upon himself all that shames and disgraces her. Faith, or better, trust is the inevitable result of such love and it frees the bride from self-preoccupation to go out into the world of the neighbor.

The world of the neighbor comprises much of the second part of the treatise. The one freed in Christ is now bound to the needs of others. Note carefully that one of words that Luther uses to link freedom and service is "flows": "From faith there flows a love and joy in the Lord" and "the good that flows from Christ flows into us . . . the good we receive from Christ flows toward those who have need of it." The image is a fountain of God's love, spilling over the sides and beyond any walls meant to contain it. It saturates all in its path, including us, and then flows through us to the neighbor in need. This love, like water itself, seeks the low places. Luther says it extends to the ungrateful. This love no longer distinguishes between friends and enemies. (Imagine that!) It seeks no obligation. It flows through us, though we be unworthy vessels. And it carries us into places we would not have ventured on our own—regions inhabited by the lost, lonely, and forsaken. For one Martin Luder who became Martin Luther, the freedom of a Christian can mean nothing less.

FOR FURTHER READING

Two recent translations of *The Freedom of a Christian* are available. Both come with introductions and commentary on the text. One is *The Freedom of a Christian*, translated and introduced by Mark D. Tranvik (Minneapolis: Fortress, 2008). The other is *The Freedom of a Christian: The Annotated Luther Study Edition*, edited by Timothy Wengert (Minneapolis: Fortress, 2016). See also *On the Freedom of a Christian with Related Texts*, edited and translated, with an introduction by Tryntje Helfferich (Indianapolis: Hackett, 2013), because it includes sixteenth-century reactions to Luther's teaching on freedom from his allies and opponents.

9

Excommunication: *Exsurge Domine* (1520) and *Decet Romanum Pontificem* (1521)

RICHARD J. SERINA, JR.

THE BULL *DECET ROMANUM Pontificem* ("It is fitting that the Roman pontiff") officially excommunicated Martin Luther on January 3, 1521. Yet it barely made a ripple or evoked a response, nor did it see the light of day until later that year. It was merely the legal consequence of the June 1520 bull *Exsurge Domine*, which had cited Luther for forty-one distinct errors and had given him sixty days to renounce those errors publicly in Rome or face automatic excommunication. Luther's unwillingness to appear in Rome or to recant had already sealed his fate, ceremonially symbolized by his burning of *Exsurge Domine* in Wittenberg on December 10. In this sense, *Decet Romanum* served as the culmination of a process dating back to 1517, when Albrecht of Mainz sent a copy of the *Ninety-Five Theses* to Rome for opinion and direction. In the weeks and months that followed, a heresy trial began according to the conventions of canon law and ecclesiastical procedure, only to stall before being resumed in 1520 and leading to *Exsurge Domine*, *Decet Romanum Pontificem*, and Luther's excommunication as a "notorious" heretic.

LUTHER'S CANONICAL TRIAL

The trial of Luther effectively began in December 1517, after Albrecht of Mainz received a copy of the *Ninety-Five Theses*. Although debate continues over whether Luther posted the theses in Wittenberg or simply sent them to Albrecht of Mainz and Hieronymus Schulz, bishop of Brandenburg, it is certain that Albrecht received the theses with Luther's accompanying letter and referred the matter to two different courts for opinion: the theological faculty at the prince's provincial university in Mainz and the curia in Rome.[1] He first requested an opinion of his theology faculty—a common procedure for testing theological ideas articulated by theology professors that contested church doctrine. The medieval professor of theology had a right to dissent to teachings that were not officially settled in the church through papal decree or the decision of a council.[2] Upon the recommendation of Mainz, Albrecht also sent a copy of the theses to Rome for examination in the papal curia. This initiated a *processus inhibituros*, which would prevent the suspect theologian from continuing with his teaching on the contested matter.[3]

Medieval canon law strictly defined the nature of heresy and the process for dealing with it. The canons limited heresy to public figures who taught the faith, rather than those who simply affirmed the aberrant teaching. The heresy had to contradict Scripture as the church understood it. The false teachings had to be declared publicly rather than in private conversation or correspondence. The teacher also had to be guilty of contumacy, or adhering pertinaciously to the false doctrine when faced with correction.[4] In accordance with this, a process of jurisprudence emerged in order to treat suspected cases.[5] Consequently, Luther's foray into the criticism of indul-

---

1. On the posting of the theses, see now Volker Leppin and Timothy Wengert, "Sources for and against the Posting of the *Ninety-Five Theses*," *Lutheran Quarterly* 29 (2015): 374–98.

2. Ian Levy, "Liberty of Conscience and Freedom of Religion in the Medieval Canonists and Theologians," in *Christianity and Freedom, Volume 1: Historical Perspectives*, eds. Timothy Samuel Shah and Allen D. Hertzke (Cambridge: Cambridge University Press, 2016), 149–75.

3. Martin Brecht, *Martin Luther: His Road to the Reformation, 1483–1521*, trans. James L. Schaaf (Minneapolis: Fortress, 1985), 206 (hereafter, Brecht, *Road to Reformation*).

4. The definition of heresy is found in Gratian's *Decretum*, *Decretum Gratiani* causa 24, quaestio 3, c. 27–31, *Corpus Iuris Canonici*, ed. Emil Friedberg, 2 vols. (Leipzig: Tauchnitz, 1879), 1:998 (hereafter, Friedberg).

5. The process for prosecuting heresy, established for inquisitorial procedure, is found in the 1206 decretal *Qualiter et Quando* and in the canons of Lateran IV (1215). These were later incorporated into the Gregorian Decretals. See *Decretalium Gregorii*

gences not only proceeded according to his right as a university professor of theology, but even its prosecution had clearly defined parameters that protected this right.

The first phase of Luther's canonical trial related directly to the indulgence theses. It was initiated by Albrecht when he sent the theses to both the faculty in Mainz and to the curia in Rome. However, the case against Luther in Rome did not begin until months later, when Sylvester Prierias, the Master of the Sacred Palace or "chief theologian" in the Roman curia, responded to Luther's theses. The report, Prierias's *Dialogue concerning the Power of the Pope against the Presumptuous Opinions of Martin Luther*, argued against Luther on the basis of papal authority: if the pope as universal bishop of the church has declared indulgences according to his infallible office, then they cannot be gainsaid without questioning this infallibility, which *de facto* makes one a heretic.[6] On the basis of Prierias's opinion, Rome charged Luther with heresy in June 1518. On August 7, 1518, Luther received the *Dialogue* along with a citation of his errors and summons to appear in Rome within sixty days (no longer extant). As a result of the collaboration between Prierias and Girolamo de Ghinucci, auditor of the apostolic *camera*, the decision of Rome considered Luther guilty of heresy because his errors were "notorious," that is, made public through his writings.[7]

Through the negotiations of Luther's prince, Frederick the Wise, Rome revised the summons to Augsburg, where Luther would meet with Cardinal Cajetan (Tommaso de Vio). The Dominican theologian Cajetan had a strong reputation for his commentaries on the writings of Thomas Aquinas and for his defense of papal authority against the conciliarists of Paris during the controversy of the *conciliabulum* ("pseudo-council") of Pisa.[8] Cajetan shared some of Luther's concerns over indulgences, yet Pope Leo X prohibited Cajetan from debating Luther at Augsburg and required only that Luther recant of his teaching.[9] This was no longer a matter for

---

IX, liber V, tit. 1, c. 17 (Friedberg 2:738–39, 745–47) and liber V, tit. 1, c. 24 (Friedberg 2:745–47). For an extended discussion of the procedure as it existed in the Late Middle Ages, see Thomas A. Fudge, *The Trial of Jan Hus: Medieval Heresy and Criminal Procedure* (Oxford: Oxford University Press, 2013), esp. 73–115, and Melodie H. Eichbauer, "Rethinking Causae 23–26 as the Causae hereticorum," *Zeitschrift der Savigny-Stiftung für Rechtsgeschichte* 101 (2015): 86–149.

6. Luther's response to Prierias can be found at Martin Luther, WA 1:647–86.

7. James Atkinson, *The Trial of Luther* (New York: Stein & Day, 1971), 54 (hereafter, Atkinson, *Trial of Luther*).

8. Nelson Minnich, "The Healing of the Pisan Schism (1511–1513)," *Annuarium Historiae Conciliorum* 16 (1984): 59–192.

9. *Postquam ad aures*, dated August 23, 1518. On this, see Scott H. Hendrix, *Luther and the Papacy: Stages in a Reformation Conflict* (Philadelphia: Fortress, 1981), 65–66.

debate or private conversation. Nevertheless, Luther did not recant and the meeting devolved into a conflict over papal authority, namely, whether papal bulls had the right to establish articles of faith.[10] This effectively ended the first phase of Luther's trial, yet without resolution. Cajetan reported the outcome of the events to Frederick the Wise, requesting that Luther be sent to Rome or expelled from Electoral Saxony.[11] Cajetan later drafted a decree on indulgences for Leo X that was published in December 1518, presumably to end the controversy over the topic.[12] Yet Rome did not excommunicate Luther at this point, even though it had every reason to do so.

The second phase of Luther's trial began after an extended delay. Emperor Maximillian died in January 1519, leaving a vacuum that led to attempts by Rome to mollify the indulgence controversy in order to gain a favorable candidate to replace Maximillian. The electors finally selected Maximillian's son, Charles V, to replace him in June 1519. At the same time, Luther participated in a momentous debate with John Eck of Ingolstadt concerning, among other things, papal primacy.[13] During the course of the debate, Luther defended his rejection of papal primacy by divine right with recourse to the Greeks and Bohemians, who he argued were still Christians despite the fact that they rejected primacy. In response to criticism from Eck, Luther stated that, though the Council of Constance in 1415 had excommunicated and executed the Bohemian theologian Jan Hus, many of Hus's teachings were "most Christian and evangelical."[14] Eck accused Luther of denying the infallibility of councils by defending Hus. To that, Luther famously responded that councils, like popes, could err and had erred, and that they had no right to establish new articles of faith. Reports of the debate reignited the controversy over the *causa Lutheri*. The universities at Cologne and Louvain condemned Luther for his views articulated at Leipzig, while Eck sent a letter to Rome celebrating his self-declared victory.[15]

---

10. See Suzanne Hequet, "The 1518 Proceedings at Augsburg," *Lutheran Quarterly* 32 (2018): 60–70.

11. Brecht, *Road to the Reformation*, 261.

12. Ultimately published in January 1519 as the bull *Cum postquam*. For Luther's response, LW 48:105.

13. On Leipzig, see Kurt K. Hendel, "The 1519 Leipzig Debate," *Lutheran Quarterly* 32 (2018): 446–54; and Mickey Mattox, Richard J. Serina Jr., and Jonathan Mumme, eds., *Luther at Leipzig: Martin Luther, the Leipzig Debate, and the Sixteenth-Century Reformations* (Leiden: Brill, 2019) (hereafter, *Luther at Leipzig*).

14. The text of the Leipzig Debate is at WA 59:427–605. For a recent translation of selected portions, see Carl D. Roth and Richard J. Serina Jr., "The Disputation between John Eck and Martin Luther (1519): A Select Translation," in *Luther at Leipzig*, 321–43.

15. Brecht, *Road to the Reformation*, 348.

The Leipzig Debate raised a new issue that the first phase of Luther's canonical trial had not addressed directly and would predominate in the second phase: the challenge to church authority—both pope and council. During the controversy over indulgences, many of Luther's critics dealt less with the theology of indulgences than with the authority of the pope to institute indulgences, as Prierias had. Luther had no intention of debating the authority of the papacy and did so only in response to his opponents. With the Leipzig Debate, however, church authority emerged as the primary target of Luther's teaching and the impetus for his eventual excommunication. But it again happened in fits and starts. The case against Luther was reopened on January 9, 1520, at the instigation of an anonymous Italian critic during a public consistory.[16] Two days later, Pope Leo X sent a letter to Frederick the Wise denouncing the prince's support for Luther. On February 1, 1520, Leo convened a commission and charged them with preparing an official denunciation. The commission included Cajetan, a canon lawyer in Cardinal Pietro Accolti, and several representatives of mendicant orders, mostly Observant Franciscans.[17] The commission was to make a formal investigation and draw up a list of errors. However, by February 11, 1520, changes were made because the mendicant members had not been up to the task. They were subsequently replaced by another noted antagonist of Luther in Prierias.[18]

The final impetus for the bull of excommunication came with the arrival of Eck at Rome in late March 1520. Eck immediately inserted himself into the process. Leo X appointed a third commission to draft the bull of excommunication, which now included Cajetan, Accolti, a Spanish theologian at the Sapienza University in Rome (identified only as Johannes Hispanus), and Eck.[19] They were supposed to review a draft of the bull by Accolti, but Eck convinced the commission to expand the bull, citing and condemning Luther explicitly as a heretic on forty-one different counts. Initially, Cajetan had planned to treat each error on its own merits, ranging from "erroneous" to "heretical"—two very different technical designations.[20] Eck won the day

16. Brecht, *Road to the Reformation*, 389.

17. Peter Fabisch, "Johannes Eck und die Publikationen der Bullen *Exsurge Domine* und *Decet Romanum Pontificem*," in *Johannes Eck (1486–1543) im Streit der Jahrhunderte*, ed. Erwin Iserloh (Münster: Aschendorf, 1988), 77 (hereafter, Fabisch, "Johannes Eck").

18. Atkinson, *Trial of Luther*, 82.

19. Brecht, *Road to the Reformation*, 390.

20. Remigius Bäumer, "Der Lutherprozess," in *Lutherprozess und Lutherbann: Vorgeschichte, Ergebnis, Nachwirkung*, ed. Remigius Bäumer (Münster: Aschendorff, 1972), 36 (hereafter, Bäumer, "Der Lutherprozess").

and eventually submitted his revision of the bull to Leo X on May 2, who then had it presented to the college of cardinals for discussion in four different consistories on May 21, May 23, May 25, and June 1.[21] The bull, titled *Exsurge Domine*, ultimately passed and was promulgated by Leo on June 15 and posted at St. Peter's on July 24, accompanied by a bonfire of Luther's works.

Over the next two months, the curia's appointed representatives Hieronymus Aleander, papal librarian, and John Eck were sent to publish *Exsurge Domine* in German lands. They served it to select princes, bishops, and universities throughout the Holy Roman Empire, but not to all. Eck, interestingly enough, had the responsibility of posting the bull in Luther's territory. He discharged that duty in Brandenburg on September 29, but was hesitant to enter Wittenberg. On October 3, he sent the bull to Wittenberg via courier—possibly a militiaman—because he was afraid of the response were he to deliver it by hand.[22] Luther received the bull on October 10, thereby putting into effect the 60 days for him to appear in Rome and recant of his teachings. Two days later, Luther reluctantly met with the German papal secretary Karl von Miltitz, who for a second time during the process sought to ease the tensions.[23] He advised Luther to write a letter to the pope, which he would date September 6—before the bull was published—and in which he would target Eck as the source of the controversy. Nevertheless, Luther busied himself responding to the bull. Since *Exsurge Domine* implicated others beyond Luther, and since the bull came with civil penalties to be implemented by the secular authorities within the Holy Roman Empire, there was need to take preemptive legal action. In addition to Luther himself, Eck had arranged to implicate a number of other supporters in the bull, including Wittenberg colleagues Andreas Bodenstein von Karlstadt and Johannes Doletz of Feldkirchen, the Zwickau preacher Johannes Sylvius Egranus, humanist cathedral canon Bernhard Adelmann of Augsburg, and humanists Willibald Pirckheimer and Lazarus Spengler of Nuremberg.[24] Both Luther and Karlstadt appealed to a council over the next month.[25] In fact, Luther's own appeal was purportedly made to protect his colleagues at Wittenberg.[26] Luther had hoped the city of Wittenberg would join in the

---

21. Bäumer, "Der Lutherprozess," 36.

22. Brecht, *Road to the Reformation*, 401.

23. This resulted in the "Open Letter to Pope Leo" introducing *Freedom of a Christian* at WA 7:42–49; LW 31:334–343.

24. Bäumer, "Der Lutherprozess," 46.

25. Brecht, *Road to the Reformation*, 415.

26. Brecht, *Road to the Reformation*, 405; see also WA Br 2:195.27–32.

official appeal, but the council declined.[27] Luther also began to write against the bull. In November, he drafted a treatise against Eck (*Eck's New Bull and Lies*) and another against the bull in Latin (*Against the Execrable Bull of the Antichrist*), later composing an expanded German version against the bull (*Against the Bull of the Antichrist*).[28]

Then, on December 10, 1520, Luther famously burned the bull threatening excommunication in Wittenberg, when the sixty-day period for appearance and repentance had expired. The students burned a host of other texts, including the books of canon law, the *Summa Angelica* (a manual for confessors composed by the fifteenth-century Franciscan Angelus de Clavasio), and the writings of Luther's principal opponents, including Eck and Emser. Incidentally, students would not part with the writings of Aquinas or Duns Scotus. Finally, in dramatic fashion, Luther laid *Exsurge Domine* on the smoldering fire, and the crowd dispersed. This burning of the bull, of course, was not unprovoked. Not only had Rome burned Luther's books, but Charles V had ordered their burning in Louvain and Lüttich. His books were also burned in Merseburg, Meissen, Cologne, and Mainz upon the publication of *Exsurge Domine*. Luther later went on to explain further his rationale for the book burning in a December treatise (*Why the Books of the Pope, and His Disciples Were Burned by Doctor Martin Luther*) and a more extensive reply to the bull at the behest of Frederick, first in Latin (*Defense of All the Articles of Martin Luther Condemned by the Recent Bull of Leo X*), and later a German treatment in March 1521 (*Ground and Reason for All the Articles Wrongly Condemned by the Roman Bull*).[29] Nevertheless, that Luther failed to comply with the bull's stipulations within the stated sixty days meant that he was guilty of the errors cited therein and was *de facto* a notorious and contumacious heretic to be expunged from the church.

Consequently, the bull *Decet Romanum Pontificem*, issued by Leo X on January 3, 1521, was a mere formality. Luther later referred to this as his second of a threefold excommunication: the release from his monastic vows by Johann von Staupitz, the condemnation of his views in the papal bulls, and the eventual interdict placed upon him with Charles V's Edict of Worms in May 1521.[30] Luther was by his own admission guilty of the errors cited in *Exsurge Domine*—even though he did not consider them errors. Charles V had already withdrawn Luther's invitation to speak at the

27. Brecht, *Road to the Reformation*, 414.

28. These are found at WA 6:579–94; WA 6:597–612; and WA 6:614–29.

29. These are found at WA 7:161–82; LW 31:379–95. WA 7:94–151 and WA 7:308–456; LW 32:3–99.

30. WA TR 1:442.1–5, no. 884.

coming imperial Diet of Worms once the sixty days for the Wittenberger to respond had passed. The official bull of excommunication was executed by the pope's cousin, Giulio de Medici, on January 28.[31] It took months, however, before it was published due to the presence of certain names Aleander wanted redacted.[32] In January, Spengler and Pirckheimer publicly recanted of associating with Luther's errors cited in *Exsurge*.[33] But for Luther the case was already closed. He had no intention of recanting what *Exsurge Domine* alleged against him, as he makes clear by reiterating his stance at the Diet of Worms in April 1521. On the contrary, by this time he had gone much further than the errors identified in the 1520 bull. The 1520 treatises, including *Against the Papacy at Rome, Address to the Christian Nobility*, and *Babylonian Captivity of the Church*, denounced the pope as antichrist, denied papal primacy by human right (let alone divine right), accused Rome of rejecting Scripture and councils, and contested established theological opinions on the sacraments.

In sum, the excommunication of Luther in January 1521 brought to a resolution the process begun in December 1517, which included two distinct phases addressing two different spheres of cited errors and using the terminology and procedures for the deposition of heretics practiced in the medieval ecclesiastical courts.

TEXT

Like all papal decrees, *Exsurge Domine* takes its name from the first Latin words ("Arise, O Lord"—a frequent refrain in the Psalter, but in this case a direct citation from Psalm 74:22, "Arise, O Lord, and defend your cause").[34] The bull begins with an appeal to papal authority, in particular Petrine primacy, which proves significant since the catalyst for Luther's condemnation had to do with the views on church authority he articulated at Leipzig. It also appeals to German interests, detailing not only the *translatio imperii* (the transfer of the empire from the Greeks to the Romans, and then from the Romans to the Franks with the crowning of Charlemagne as *imperator Romanorum* on Christmas Day 800), but also the recurring conflict between Bohemians and Germans, implying that Luther betrayed his countrymen with his approval of a Bohemian like Hus.

31. Fabisch, "Johannes Eck," 104.

32. Fabisch, "Johannes Eck," 105.

33. Brecht, *Road to the Reformation*, 415.

34. The bull is found in *Concilia Germaniae*, ed. Johann Friedrich Schannat and Joseph Hartzheim (Cologne: Krakamp & Simon, 1765), 6:171–79 (hereafter, CG).

What makes *Exsurge Domine* all the more notable, however, is its condemnation of Luther's errors. The bull cites forty-one errors drawn—some accurately, some inaccurately—from Luther's published writings and his public disputations. The errors divide into several different categories and proceed rather chronologically through Luther's career to that point. Errors 1–13 deal primarily with Luther's opinions on penance, sin, and confession, most of which he had addressed in the indulgence theses themselves; 14–15 address views on the Eucharist he had raised subsequently; 16–24 concern arguments he made later in the course of the indulgence controversy concerning the *thesaurus meritorum*, indulgences, and excommunication; 26–30 involve his views of the keys, papacy, and councils, as he had articulated them in Leipzig; and 31–41 include a miscellany of items that had come out after Leipzig, including good works, the burning of heretics, war against the Turks, free will, purgatory, and mendicancy.

The most pivotal of these, and those that reflect the second phase of Luther's canonical trial most directly, come from his views of church authority:

25. The Roman Pontiff, the successor of Peter, is not the vicar of Christ over all the churches of the entire world, instituted by Christ Himself in blessed Peter.

26. The word of Christ to Peter: "Whatsoever you shall loose on earth," etc., is extended merely to those things bound by Peter himself.

27. It is certain that it is not in the power of the Church or the pope to decide upon the articles of faith, and much less concerning the laws for morals or for good works.

28. If the pope with a great part of the Church thought so and so, he would not err; still it is not a sin or heresy to think the contrary, especially in a matter not necessary for salvation, until one alternative is condemned and another approved by a general Council.

29. A way has been made for us for weakening the authority of councils, and for freely contradicting their actions, and judging their decrees, and boldly confessing whatever seems true, whether it has been approved or disapproved by any council whatsoever.

30. Some articles of John Hus, condemned in the Council of Constance, are most Christian, wholly true and evangelical; these the universal Church could not condemn.[35]

---

35. CG 6:173. For an English translation, I follow the one available online at: https://www.papalencyclicals.net/leo10/l10exdom.htm.

The majority of Luther's positions addressed earlier in the bull were carried out largely in his office as doctor of theology, and thus could be granted a degree of latitude for purposes of debate and clarification. These six cited errors concerning papal authority shared a different character. Since medieval canon law had long understood heretics subject to excommunication as those unwilling to submit to church authority, or contumacious, Luther's questioning of that same church authority brought his prosecution to a head. Furthermore, nearly each of these errors is cited verbatim from statements Luther had made at Leipzig in the debate with Eck—another indication of the Ingolstadt theologian's role in incriminating his opponent.

Scholarship has dealt at length with the sources and accuracy of these cited errors. Many were inaccurate interpretations of what Luther said, conflations of what he had said at different times, or outright misquotations. At least 12 of the 41 supposed opinions of Luther failed to cite him accurately.[36] For instance, 16 reads: "It seems to have been decided that the Church in common council established that the laity should communicate under both species; the Bohemians who communicate under both species are not heretics, but schismatics." In fact, Luther had argued in his December 1519 sermon on the sacrament only that a council should rule on it, not that one had.[37] One potential reason for these inaccuracies may be the specious sources for them. Cajetan no doubt had firsthand knowledge of Luther's views from the interaction with him in Augsburg, but the majority of those cited came from two sources: the condemnations of Luther by the faculty at Louvain and Eck's own writings against and recollections of Luther's thought. At least five errors are cited verbatim from Eck's writings against Luther, while another six also appeared in the Louvain condemnation.[38] In each of these cases, the impetus came from the Leipzig Debate. Louvain had condemned Luther's opinions expressed at Leipzig, while Eck had been Luther's opponent there.

The remainder of the bull spells out the implications of Luther's continued intransigence. First, any further interaction with the works of Luther was forbidden. No one was allowed to "read, assert, preach, praise, print, publish, or defend" his works, nor to advocate for his positions "personally or through another or others, directly or indirectly, tacitly or explicitly, publicly or [secretly], either in their own homes or in other public or private

36. Hans Joachim Hillerbrand, "Martin Luther and the Bull *Exsurge Domine*," *Theological Studies* 30 (1969): 108–12.

37. See "The Blessed Sacrament of the Holy and True Body of Christ," at WA 2:742–58; LW 35:49–73.

38. Fabisch, "Johannes Eck," 81.

places."[39] Returning to Luther himself, the bull details the consequences for him. It maintains that Rome gave him every opportunity to recant of his teachings and repent of wrongdoing. Then it specifically notes that he remains "contumacious" (*contumax*)—specific technical terminology for the legal determination of heresy.[40] It also accuses him of running afoul of the 1460 bull *Execrabilis*, which Pope Pius II had issued to prohibit appeals from the decisions of popes to future councils and which Pope Julius II had affirmed against the Pisan *conciliabulum* of 1511.[41]

Exsurge Domine offers a final canonical alternative for Luther and his supporters. The bull claims that Rome has full authority to excommunicate Luther "without any further citation or delay" because of what has already been established about him as "notoriously suspect" (*notorie suspectum*) and a "true heretic." Nevertheless, it allows for Luther to remain within the church provided he "turn away from" and "abstain from his pernicious errors." Luther, along with all those "adhering to him" and "sheltering and supporting him," can avail themselves of this option by providing "legal documents" (*per legitima documenta. . .certificaverint*) to assure their compliance.[42] Finally, it gives them sixty days from the posting of the bull to provide this legal documentation (*per publica documenta in forma juris valida*)—or simply come to Rome (*si ad Nos venire voluerit, quod magis placeret*).[43] Any questions about the accuracy of the bull or Luther's orthodoxy were moot. *Exsurge Domine* proceeds on the assumption that Luther's guilt has been established and his excommunication inevitable. Like Augsburg, Luther is given only one option if he wishes to stay within the church: recant. Unlike Augsburg, however, there is on record a public citation of his errors as a notorious heretic and the threat of imminent excommunication. With the publication of *Decet Romanum Pontificem* in January 1521, Rome made good on that threat.

COMMENTARY

Three points stand out regarding Luther's excommunication and the events precipitating it. First, the two different phases of the trial correspond to two conflicting jurisdictions. The first phase of the trial dealt specifically with

39. CG 6:176.

40. CG 6:177.

41. For *Execrabilis*, see C. M. D. Crowder, *Unity, Heresy, and Reform 1378–1460: The Conciliar Response to the Great Schism* (London: Edward Yarnold, 1977), 179–81.

42. CG 6:176.

43. CG 6:177.

errors in the indulgence theses. As a duly graduated and commissioned professor of theology, Luther had the right to contest theological opinions and ecclesiastical practice, at least within reason (which is to say, unless an established teaching of the church had ruled out the opinion articulated by the theologian).[44] In the case of the indulgence theses, the proper authorities for examining and ruling on whether or not Luther had run afoul of established teaching were theological faculties (whether his own or another, such as Mainz); his local ordinaries (Albrecht and Schulz, but only at the direction of their faculties); and his religious superiors (his Augustinian Eremite prior, Staupitz, among others within his order). When Albrecht sent the theses to Rome, he thereby preempted the process within these subsidiary jurisdictions and initiated a canonical trial for alleged errors that were not necessarily under the purview of Rome. The second phase of the trial, initiated after Leipzig, led directly to the bull of excommunication owing to the influence of Eck, as well as the judgment from Louvain (and, by extension, Cologne). Once Luther began to question the authority of pope and council, this raised the profile of his arguments beyond debatable topics to matters that teachers of theology were not permitted to contest. It is in this sense that Robert McNally called Luther's trial a "failure in subsidiarity."[45] To speculate counterfactually, had the indulgence controversy never escalated to Rome, Luther may not have been drawn into debates about papal authority in response to Prierias or in the interview with Cajetan, let alone in his disputation with Eck.

Second, no one figure played a more pivotal role in Luther's excommunication than Eck, nor did any one event more than the disputation at Leipzig. It was Eck who drew Luther into a debate about papal primacy at Leipzig. Eck would report on the debate's outcome and his self-declared victory to the pope. Eck then made his way to Rome in time to redirect the drafting of the bull, landing himself a spot on the final commission. Finally, Eck had a hand in shifting the bull's citation of errors from a sliding scale to a categorical denunciation. Were it not for Eck, not only would there have been no Leipzig Debate, but there would have been no public challenge by Luther to papal authority or conciliar authority. It was this challenge that Louvain and Cologne responded to. It was this challenge that Eck reported. It was this challenge that comprised the pivotal citations 25–30 concerning church authority in *Exsurge Domine*. The person of Eck and the debate at

44. On Luther's status as a theologian, see Richard J. Serina, Jr., "Luther's Doctorate and the Start of the Reformation," *Lutheran Forum* 56:3 (2017): 53–57.

45. Robert Edwin McNally, "The Roman Process of Martin Luther: A Failure in Subsidiarity," in *The Once and Future Church: A Communion of Freedom*, ed. James A. Corriden (New York: Alba House, 1971), 111–28.

Leipzig are not only inextricably linked, but were in large part responsible for the final shape of the bull threatening excommunication and the inevitable break it effected.

Third, there is the broader question of Luther's excommunication and its ultimate importance for the Reformation. As Elisabeth Vodola has argued, in the Middle Ages excommunication shifted away from the realm of penance to the realm of law, and in so doing lost its spiritual effectiveness.[46] This is why in his earlier writings Luther can distinguish between ecclesiastical excommunication from the external church and membership in the internal church—because excommunication from the external church was strictly a legal affair.[47] Now there were strict canonical regulations governing the process, a distant bureaucracy making impersonal decisions, an endless loop of appeals, and civil penalties attached to what was once a strictly ecclesial affair. All this is to say there was nothing "final" about Luther's excommunication, as the subsequent negotiations between Charles V and the German princes revealed. The excommunication did not end Luther's public teaching or the spread of the Reformation, nor did it prevent him from receiving the sacrament or being married or buried in a Christian church. These consequences depended ultimately upon who chose to recognize and enforce the excommunication, and such decisions only served to widen the cleft between the parties.

46. Elisabeth Vodola, *Excommunication in the Middle Ages* (Berkeley: University of California Press, 1986).

47. *Sermon on the Power of Excommunication*, WA 1:638–43.

10

The Edict of Worms (1521)

THEODOR DIETER

ON JUNE 15, 1520, Pope Leo X issued the bull *Exsurge Domine* and named forty-one sentences that had been taken from Luther's writings and which Luther was now to revoke.[1] Not all quotations were correct,[2] and the sentences were torn from their context. They address indulgences, purgatory, penance, sin, faith in the sacraments, the treasure of the church, papacy, and the freedom of the will. The censure at the ends says: We "condemn, reprobate, and reject completely each of these theses or errors as either heretical, scandalous, false, offensive to pious ears or seductive of simple minds, and against Catholic truth."[3] It is not clear which kind of criticism refers to which theses. In any case, the errors are condemned, and all the faithful are obliged to regard those theses "as condemned, reprobated, and rejected."[4] Luther is asked to recant these errors publicly within sixty days of

1. *Dokumente zur Causa Lutheri (1517–1521), part 2: Vom Augsburger Reichstag 1518 bis zum Wormser Edikt 1521*, eds. Peter Fabisch and Erwin Iserloh (Münster: Aschendorff, 1991), 364–411 (hereafter cited as Fabisch/Iserloh). Parts of the bull are translated into English: https://www.papalencyclicals.net/Leo10/l10exdom.htm/.

2. See Heinrich Roos, "Die Quellen der Bulle 'Exsurge Domine,'" in *Theologie in Geschichte und Gegenwart*, eds. Johann Auer and Hermann Volk (Munich: Karl Zink, 1957), 909–26; Hans Joachim Hillerbrand, "Martin Luther and the Bull *Exsurge Domine*," *Theological Studies* 30 (1969): 108–12.

3. Fabisch/Iserloh, 388.

4. Fabisch/Iserloh, 388.

the publication of the bull. Should Luther refuse to do so, he and his follow-ers should be declared notorious heretics and their memory erased from the community of Christians. No one would be allowed to have fellowship with him; rather, he and his followers were to be taken prisoner and delivered to the Roman see. But instead of recanting, Luther defended and sharpened his views, and eventually he burnt the bull on December 10, 1520.

Thus, the excommunication of Luther became effective on January 3, 1521, through the bull *Decet Romanum Pontificem*.[5] The pope, as the su-preme judge of the church, had pronounced his judgment on Luther; now it was up to the emperor and the princes to execute this judgment. According to the laws of the Holy Roman Empire of the German Nation, each eccle-sial excommunication had to be followed by the corresponding measures by the temporal authorities. The newly elected emperor (June 25, 1519), crowned on October 23, 1520, was now in the center of the question of how the ban against Luther would be executed in the German empire. The first of six questions that the electoral prince of Cologne asked him at the solemn coronation in Aachen was: whether he was prepared to preserve the tradi-tional faith, protect the church and clergy, show reverence and devotion to the pope and the Roman Church. Also in all other ruler's oaths, which he had already sworn when he took possession of the other parts of his great empire, he publicly committed himself to protect the church and the true faith.[6] In the territories where he was a sovereign ruler writings of the her-etic Luther were burnt, as in the Netherlands, in Liège, Louvain, later in his presence also in Aachen after his coronation, in Cologne and in Mainz in November 1520. In Germany, Charles was dependent on the cooperation of the electoral princes, the other princes, and the magistrates of the imperial cities; thus, he needed to seek consensus with them, or at least be cautious if he wanted to impose his will on them. This constellation full of tensions determined the Diet, which the emperor opened in Worms on January 28, 1521, and which lasted until May 25.

In his election agreement, Charles had promised that the edict of outlawry would not be imposed on a man or a city without them being heard, and an inhabitant of the empire would not be brought before a for-eign court. In a letter to the emperor, the Saxon electoral prince, wishing to protect Luther, wrote:

> My request that nothing be done against Luther before he has
> been heard is made for the purpose that the truth and whether

5. Fabisch/Iserloh, 435–67.

6. Heinz Schilling, *Karl V.: Der Kaiser, dem die Welt zerbrach* (Munich: Beck, 2020), 101 (hereafter cited as Schilling, *Karl V.*).

> Luther is wrong in his writings may come to light, for Luther has
> offered to come here with safe conduct and to be interrogated by
> equal-ranking, honorable, and impartial judges and, where he
> would be overcome by Scripture, to be submissively rebuked.[7]

This request seemed to be a natural course of action, in normal legal proceedings, but not in this case. The verdict had already been pronounced, and by the highest authority on earth. If the electoral prince nevertheless demanded that a disputation be held to clarify the question of whether errors were found in Luther's writings, then, even without explicitly saying so, he was questioning the authority of the pope as the supreme guarantor of the truth of the faith. With *Decet Romanum Pontificem* the pope had declared Luther a heretic; the bull was posted on many churches in Germany, it was preached about, and yet the prince declared the matter open! The electoral prince had asked Erasmus for advice on this matter, and the latter probably told him the same thing that he wrote to the university rector after Luther's books were burned in the university city of Leuven in the wake of *Exsurge Domine*:

> I have never approved, and I never shall, the suppression of a
> man in this way, by public uproar, before his books have been
> read and discussed, before a man's errors have been pointed out
> to him, and before he has been refuted with arguments and with
> evidence from Holy Scripture . . . The burning of his books will
> perhaps banish Luther from our libraries, whether he can be
> plucked out of human beings' hearts, I am not sure.[8]

This shows that in those days papal decisions and declarations were not simply taken as the last word in a controversy.

Affirming the authority of the pope, the papal special nuncio Girolamo Aleander strongly opposed any invitation of Luther to Worms. Nevertheless, the fear of the imperial advisers was this: "A condemnation of the heretic by Charles V alone, out of his own power and on the basis of the papal bull of excommunication, would have been seen as a breach of the constitution of the empire and would have caused uproar in view of the anti-Roman mood in Germany."[9] At the time of the Diet in Worms, there were already more than 600,000 copies of Luther's works among the people. This had to be

---

7. *Deutsche Reichstagsakten unter Kaiser Karl V.*, vol. 2, ed. Adolf Wrede (Gotha: Friedrich Andreas Perthes, 1896), 471.5–11 (hereafter cited as RTA).

8. Quoted from Geoffrey Parker, *Emperor: A New Life of Charles V* (New Haven: Yale University Press, 2019), 118 (hereafter cited as Parker, *Emperor*).

9. Volker Reinhardt, *Luther der Ketzer: Rom und die Reformation* (Munich: Beck, 2016), 149.

taken seriously. Thus, despite Aleander's attempts, in a letter dated March 6, 1520, the emperor asked Luther to come to Worms.[10] In it, Luther was not addressed as a heretic, but as "Venerable, Dear, Pious."[11] The letter did not speak of a revocation, which Luther was to perform, but indicated that the estates of the Diet wanted information about the books Luther had written. Safe conduct was emphatically guaranteed, and a letter of consignment was enclosed.[12] While he could not prevent the emperor from calling Luther to Worms, Aleander had to make sure that no disputation would take place at the meeting, but that Luther would only be asked to revoke his writings. On the other side, the Saxon Elector did not take any precautions to ensure that a disputation could have taken place by impartial scholars. What he could have expected in the best case remains unclear. For Aleander, it was only a matter of a yes or a no to the demand for revocation, and he expected the latter answer. In addition, he had to prevent Luther from "misusing" the Diet for his propaganda. In fact, parallel to Luther's invitation, the imperial court prepared a mandate against him, after two drafts of such a mandate had already been rejected by the imperial estates.

Luther's journey to Worms became a triumphal procession for his cause. On April 17, he stood before the emperor and empire for the first time. Luther made a disappointing impression. To the first question asked him, whether the books before him were written by him, he answered yes; to the second question, whether he would revoke the views expressed in them, he reacted hesitantly and uncertainly, asking for time to think about them. This was a surprise to all who were present at the interrogation, but in view of the letter of invitation to the meeting, which reads differently, and Luther's repeatedly declared willingness and expectation to answer in free disputation, this may be understandable.[13] Luther's second appearance is well known. He refused to recant because his conscience was "caught" in the words (plural!) of God. Precisely because his conscience was bound by the words of God, he had to demand freedom, that is, respect for his conscience. But Luther also knew that it was *his* knowledge of the words of God that bound him, and as a human being he could err.[14] Therefore, he had to be prepared to subject his knowledge to a test. Because no disputation

10. WA Br 2:280.1–21.

11. WA Br 2:280.3.

12. WA Br 2:280.1–281.32.

13. Geoffrey Parker says that "Luther had indeed received advance notice of the two simple questions (Parker, *Emperor*, 121)," but this does not seem to be so clear. See Martin Brecht, *Martin Luther: His Road to the Reformation 1483–1521*, trans. James L. Schaaf (Minneapolis: Fortress, 1985), 453, 455.

14. WA 7:834.11–23.

had taken place in Worms, let alone any testing by a group of impartial theologians, no revocation could be expected from Luther. A revocation would have presupposed that Luther had been taught better by scriptural arguments so that he would have been able to correct his previous understanding. This became a standard legal argument of Saxon politics when it later defended Luther's refusal to recant.

Until his encounter with Luther at the Diet, Emperor Charles V did not seem determined to take consistent action against Luther. This changed at the latest during Luther's second interrogation. The next day, Charles responded with a short speech, composed by hand, regarding Luther's refusal to recant, a very impressive confession by the 21-year-old emperor.[15] He saw himself in a long line of kings and emperors, all of whom shared and defended the Church's faith, the faith that Luther attacked. Therefore he wanted to hold on to this faith in everything. And he stressed: "It is certain that a single monk errs in his opinion which is against what all of Christendom has held for over a thousand years to the present. According to his [Luther's] opinion, all of Christendom has always been in error."[16] And the emperor boldly announced: "To settle this matter I am therefore determined to use all my dominions and possessions, my friends, my body, my blood, my life and my soul."[17] Charles was convinced that he received his kingship to defend and protect the Catholic faith; this was part of the *raison d'être* of his kingship. With regard to Luther he said: "After the impertinent reply which Luther gave yesterday in our presence, I declare that I now regret having delayed so long the proceedings against him and his false doctrines. I am resolved that I will never again hear him talk."[18]

Charles recognized the need to reform the church; but, unlike Luther, for him this reform was connected with the fight against heresy as he understood it. Seven years later he said in a speech to his advisers:

> To tell the truth, the goal of my trip to Italy is to force the Pope to hold a general council in Italy or Germany, against the heresies and for the reformation of the church. I swear to God and to His Son that nothing in the world oppresses me as much as Luther's heresy and that I will do my utmost to ensure that the historians who tell of the origin of heresy in my days also add that I have done everything against it; yes, I would be reviled in this world

15. See Hans J. Hillerbrand, *The Reformation: A Narrative History Related by Contemporary Observers and Participants* (New York: Harper & Row, 1964), 94 (hereafter cited as Hillerbrand).

16. Hillerbrand, 94.

17. Hillerbrand, 94.

18. Hillerbrand, 94.

and condemned in the hereafter if I did not do everything to reform the Church and to destroy the accursed heresy.[19]

This shows the seriousness and energy of his fight against the Lutheran Reformation. Now the way was open for the nuncio Aleander to formulate the text of the edict against Luther at the Diet. The text was finished on May 8th in Latin and German. It received this date according to the notarization order of the emperor. However, the emperor did not sign the edict until May 26. He wanted to submit it to the imperial estates more for information than for approval; this did not happen until after the end of the Diet on May 25, 1521. Some princes had already left before that date, and for those estates still present, electoral prince Joachim of Brandenburg declared their approval without discussion. The date of May 8 gave the impression that the Diet had officially approved it. But the emperor could have issued the edict out of his own power. In any case, it came into being lawfully, although Luther did not agree.[20]

Before his premature departure from the Diet, Luther's electoral prince asked the emperor not to send the expected mandate against Luther to Electoral Saxony. The emperor agreed to this, and since it was not published in the very territory where Luther lived, the Edict of Worms was not put into effect there. A peculiar irony of the history of the Reformation! Certainly, Luther's freedom of movement was restricted by the edict, yet he was less affected by it than were his followers outside of Electoral Saxony. The Nuremberg Imperial Diet officially adopted the Worms edict into its final document (*Reichstagsabschied*) in 1524 and issued a mandate to execute it, but with the ambiguous addition that the estates should follow the edict "as much as possible."[21] Luther, annoyed by this, published the Worms edict as well as the Nuremberg mandate with short critical remarks.[22] In 1526, the Diet of Speyer allowed the estates to carry out the edict as they "hope and believe they can answer for it before God and imperial majesty."[23] But at the second Diet of Speyer in 1529, the majority decided that the Edict of Worms should again be strictly enforced. The estates that adhered to the Reformation protested against this and confessed that the relevant

19. Quoted from Schilling, *Karl V.*, 136.

20. For Luther's denial, see WA 19, 276,8–25; for the legal aspects, see Armin Kohnle, *Reichstag und Reformation: Kaiserliche und ständische Religionspolitik von den Anfängen der Causa Lutheri bis zum Nürnberger Religionsfrieden* (Gütersloh: Gütersloher Verlagshaus, 2001), 12–13; 100–101 (hereafter cited as Kohnle, *Reichstag*).

21. Quoted from Kohnle, *Reichstag*, 218.

22. WA 15:254–78.

23. Quoted from Kohnle, *Reichstag*, 269.

provisions concerning the edict had been passed "against God and his holy word, the salvation of all our souls and good conscience" and were therefore considered invalid by them.[24]

THE EDICT OF WORMS

The beginning of the edict resembles the confession of the emperor as his response to Luther's final statement. It is said that the imperial office has two great tasks: to enlarge the empire, inherited from the ancestors, and to keep the Christian faith pure against heresies. This responsibility is all the greater for Charles, because none of his ancestors possessed such a wealth of power. To give space to heresies would violate both the conscience and the glory of the emperor. The heresies that have arisen in Germany in the previous three years have already been condemned by councils, which of course means that they must not be debated. Thus the widespread demand to "hear" Luther, to have him present at the Diet, to offer him the opportunity to explain and defend his views in a disputation and to try to refute them, is in fact meaningless. The matter is already decided and needs no further disputation: "[I]t is plain to you all how far these errors and heresies depart from the Christian way, which a certain Martin Luther, of the Augustinian order, has sought violently and virulently to introduce and disseminate within the Christian religion."[25] The edict describes the consequences if the authorities did not fight against the heresies quickly and energetically: "disorder, and mighty dissolution and pitiable downfall of good morals, and of the peace and the Christian faith" would follow.[26]

The text then describes what the pope did; in several places in the edict one finds shorter or longer narratives about the mildness and patience with which pope and cardinals, emperor and princes treated Luther to induce him to repent. To be a heretic, one must not only publicly express opinions that conflict with the teaching of the Church, but must also, when warned of heresy, persevere with one's opinion.[27] Those reports about the proceedings against Luther have the goal to show that the Roman side did everything to preserve Luther from his road to ruin, that therefore the responsibility

24. Quoted from Heinrich Bornkamm, "Die Geburtsstunde des Protestantismus," in *Das Jahrhundert der Reformation: Gestalten und Kräfte* (Frankfurt: Insel, 1983), 160.

25. Hillerbrand, 95.

26. Hillerbrand, 95.

27. See Richard J. Serena, "The Excommunication of Martin Luther: *Exsurge Domine* (1520) and *Decet Romanum Pontificem* (1521)," *Lutheran Quarterly* 34:2 (2020): 194–208, 195.

for what is to come lies solely with Luther and that the trial against him was formally correct. The fact that Luther had not obeyed the summons to Rome and had not recanted despite many Roman efforts has made strict measures inevitable. Thus, finally, the pope declared Luther to be the "son of disobedience and wickedness and a divider and heretic who is to be avoided by all."[28] Since no formal objections can be made to the proceedings, now they are rightly cracking down on Luther. By sending the bull to them, the pope has asked the temporal authorities to execute the measures announced in it against the heretic and to fulfil their duties.

The edict complains that not even the condemnation by the bull and its execution by burning books have made Luther recant or ask for absolution; rather, he has added with his further books "bad fruits of his perverse mind and spirit."[29] This refers to "On the Babylonian Captivity of the Church." The edict here goes far beyond *Exsurge Domine* and, although it is the document of temporal authorities, it declares Luther's view of the sacraments to be heretical as deviating from tradition (Lateranense IV). It mentions Luther's denial that there are seven sacraments, his "defilement" of the "indissoluble bond of marriage," his understanding of last unction as a "mere invention," communion under both forms as with the Bohemians, the problematization of confession so that it can no longer give comfort to burdened hearts, his contempt for the priestly office and his "scurrilous and shameful words" against the successor of Peter.[30] And he denies free will. The mass confers benefit only on those who take part in it, not on the deceased.[31]

> Especially does he impugn the authority of the holy fathers, as they are received by the Church, and would destroy obedience and authority of every kind. Indeed, he writes nothing which does not arouse and promote sedition, discord, war, murder, robbery and arson, and tend toward the complete downfall of the Christian faith. For he teaches a loose, self-willed life, severed from all laws and wholly brutish; and he is a loose, self-willed man, who condemns and rejects all laws; for he has shown no fear or shame in burning publicly the decretals and canon law.[32]

28. RTA 2:645.10–11.

29. RTA 2:646.3–4.

30. Hillerbrand, 98.

31. Hillerbrand's translation of this sentence (98) is incorrect: "And he writes that the mass confers no benefit on him for whom it is celebrated."

32. Hillerbrand, 98.

Aleander had tried to show the imperial estates that Luther's teaching would lead to turmoil and discord. To avoid such conflicts was an outstanding concern of all participants in the Diet. The repeated indication that a harsh action against Luther could lead to an uprising of the "common man" might have served for some as a proof of Aleander's opinion while others would blame the Roman side for instigating the violence.

Particularly serious for many of Luther's contemporaries was his denial of the authority of councils. When Luther stated in Worms, in his closing words at the second interrogation, that councils have erred, Charles V interrupted the imperial orator Johann von Eck and finished the interrogation: "That is enough: I do not wish to hear any more from someone who denied the authority of the councils!"[33] Luther had appealed to a council, and the emperor had tried to urge the pope to hold a council; but if even the authority of councils was fundamentally in question, what sense would this make? Who then could be the judge in this conflict? Luther's general criticism of councils and of the Council of Constance in particular is especially emphasized in the edict.

The edict sees Luther "not as a human being, but as the evil enemy in the form of a man in a monk's habit."[34] Nevertheless, it is emphasized that the emperor and the Diet dealt with Luther with great patience and without applying the procedural rules in all their severity. This is described in detail: the gracious invitation to the *Reichstag*, the granting of a period of reflection after the first interrogation, the second interrogation with the refusal to recant, then three days of negotiations with Luther in small circles until the heretic's departure.[35]

Before the measures against Luther and his followers are made known, the fact of his heresy and the judgment about him are stated: "Martin Luther still persists obstinately and perversely in maintaining his heretical opinions, and consequently all pious and God-fearing persons abominate and abhor him as one mad or possessed by a demon."[36] The edict is issued in praise of God, the protection of the Christian faith and the honor of the pope (as to goal) by virtue of the imperial office and its authority (as to competence) with the unanimous approval of the Diet for the execution of the judgment which the pope has proclaimed with the bull on Luther (as to object). With the edict, the emperor determined how Luther was to be regarded by all: "as a limb cut off from the Church of God, an obstinate schismatic and manifest

33. Quoted from Parker, *Emperor*, 122.
34. RTA 2:648.10–11.
35. RTA 2:648–52.
36. Hillerbrand, 99.

heretic."[37] This is followed by the threat of punishment in case the provisions of the edict were violated. Afterwards the measures follow first against Luther, then against his followers, further against his books and those sharing his opinions.

> We strictly order that [. . .] you shall refuse to give the aforesaid Martin Luther hospitality, lodging, food, or drink; neither shall anyone, by word or deed, secretly or openly, succour or assist him by counsel or help; but in whatever place you meet him, you shall proceed against him; if you have sufficient force, you shall take him prisoner and keep him in close custody; you shall deliver him, or cause him to be delivered, to us or at least let us know where he may be captured. In the meanwhile you shall keep him closely imprisoned until you receive notice from us what further to do, according to the direction of the laws. And for such holy and pious work we will indemnify you for your trouble and expense.[38]

Luther is made an outlaw, cut off not only from the ecclesial but also from the secular community. He should be captured if possible, but no license to kill is granted. It would then be up to the ecclesial and temporal authorities to decide what to do with a captured Luther.

> In like manner you shall proceed against his friends, adherents, patrons, maintainers, abettors [. . .] and followers. And the property of these, whether personal or real, you shall, in virtue of the sacred ordinances and of our imperial ban and over-ban, treat in this way; namely, you shall attack and overthrow its possessors and wrest their property from them and transfer it to your own custody and uses; and no one shall hinder or impede these measures, unless the owner shall abandon his unrighteous way and secure papal absolution.[39]

The prospect of being able to appropriate and use the property of the outlaws was of course a strong motive to take action against these people. The protection of property belonging to a community does not apply to those who have been excluded from the community.

> Consequently we command you, each and all, under the penalties already prescribed, that henceforth no one shall dare to buy, sell, read, preserve, copy, print, or cause to be copied or

37. Hillerbrand, 99.
38. Hillerbrand, 99.
39. Hillerbrand, 99–100.

printed, any books of the aforesaid Martin Luther, condemned
by our holy father the Pope as aforesaid, or any other writings
in German or Latin hitherto composed by him, since they are
foul, harmful, suspected, and published by a notorious and stiff-
necked heretic. Neither shall any dare to approve his opinions,
nor to proclaim, defend, or assert them, in any other way that
human ingenuity can invent, notwithstanding he may have put
some good in them to deceive the simple man.[40] [The text continues:] For just as the very best food, when mixed with a drop
of poison, is shunned by all human beings, how much more
shall such writings and books, in which so much poison for
souls and damnation is contained, not only be shunned by all of
us, but also be removed from the memory of all human beings
and destroyed, so that they can harm no one or kill eternally.
For all what has been well written in his [Luther's] books, was
already formerly indicated many times by the holy fathers, who
were accepted and approved by the Church. There it can be read
and held without having to worry or be suspicious of any evil.[41]

It is thus well recognized that in Luther's writings some good insights
are to be found, but this good does not cancel out the bad; rather, the poison
for the soul contained therein does not permit Luther's books to be read
because of the good in them. These books, and with them their fatal ideas,
shall be completely erased from the memory of human beings. Here, then,
we are concerned with a *damnatio memoriae* ("condemnation of memory") not of Luther's person, rather of his books and ideas. To this end, the
emperor commands all worldly authorities in his domain, under threat of
punishment, to order in their area of responsibility that "Luther's poisoned
writings and books, because they cause so much turmoil, damage, division
and heresy in the Church of God, are to be burned with fire, or in one way
or another completely removed, destroyed and annihilated."[42]

The thoughts of Luther may also not be spread by other authors. No
books may be written, printed, painted, sold or purchased which contain
anything "which gives rise to error in our holy faith and contradicts what
the holy Christian Church has hitherto held, as well as hostile writings and
calumnies against our holy father, the pope, prelates, princes, high schools
and their faculties and other honorable persons, and what leads away from
good morals and the holy Roman Church."[43] Thus, any criticism of the

40. Hillerbrand, 100.
41. RTA 2:655.23–32.
42. RTA 2:656.6–9.
43. RTA 2:657.5–10.

Church is prohibited. A special commandment goes to the judicial authorities, who are to ensure that the aforementioned prohibition is enforced.

A censorship provision follows. In drafting the edict, Aleander was proud that he had in this way, without being allowed to name it, introduced the bull *Inter sollicitudines* of May 4, 1515,[44] into imperial law.[45] "No printer [. . .] may begin to print books or writings containing anything that concerns the Christian faith to a lesser or greater extent without the consent of the local bishop or his representative or deputy and without the consent of the theological faculty of one of the nearest universities."[46] This censorship provision also applies to all other books, whatever their contents, which may be printed only with the consent of at least the local bishop or his deputy. This will be a threat to all printers in the future.

The Edict of Worms ends with the words: "So that all that [has been determined in the edict] may be realized and believed, we have sealed this letter with the imperial seal. The letter is given in our and the Holy Kingdom city of Worms, on May 8th of the 1521st year after Christ's birth, the second year of our Roman Empire and the sixth year of all [our] other empires."[47]

COMMENTARY

By its origin, the Edict of Worms became a document of the crisis of church authority. With the bull *Decet Romanum Pontificem* Luther was expelled from the church because of heresy. This was a decision of the highest ecclesial judge, but this decision was not, as was to be expected according to the law, automatically followed by the emperor making Luther an outlaw; rather, the Saxon electoral prince demanded to "hear" Luther in Worms in order to bring the truth about him to light. Simply by doing so they called into question the authority of the Roman judgment. The frequent abuse of the heresy accusation in the Middle Ages had already contributed to this loss of authority. "After all, the exercise of ecclesiastical teaching authority was used early on as a means of fighting all kinds of opponents—for example in disputes between monks and overly free teachers, between world clergy and mendicants, between Dominicans and Franciscans and within

44. See *Quellen zur Geschichte des Papsttums und des Römischen Katholizismus*, eds. Carl Mirbt (1st—5th edition) and Kurt Aland (6th, completely revised edition), vol. 1 (Tübingen: Mohr/Siebeck, 1967), 497 (no. 784).

45. Fabisch/Iserloh, 542f., fn. 58.

46. RTA 2:658.2–9.

47. RTA 2:658.24–659.2.

the mendicant orders."[48] The papal nuncio Aleander wrote in a letter on February 8, 1521: "But now all Germany is in great turmoil; nine tenths are raising the field cry 'Luther!', and for the remaining tenth, if they are indifferent to Luther, the slogan is at least: 'Death to the Roman court!'"[49] Even though this may be exaggerated, the mere fact that so many people shared Luther's ideas, which the Roman magisterium had declared to be heretical, demonstrates how many had emigrated from the domain of papal authority. Under these circumstances it would not lead to conflict resolution simply to appeal or refer to papal authority. Thus, many participants of the Diet in Worms were in favor of offering a hearing to Luther as eventually happened in April of 1521. Even if finally Nuncio Aleander formulated the edict in the sense of *Exsurge Domine* and *Decet Romanum Pontificem*, the fact that it did not come into force in Electoral Saxony where Luther lived shows that the doubts about papal authority and the opposition to it could not be removed by the threat of violence.

This crisis of authority is reflected in the ambiguity and even self-contradiction of the demand that Luther should be "heard" at the Diet. On February 19, 1521, the imperial estates rejected the draft of an imperial mandate against Luther and demanded, with a view to the "common man," that Luther should appear at the Diet with safe conduct and be "heard" by some learned and knowledgeable people. The theological conflict was by no means to be disputed; Luther was only to be asked whether he wanted to insist on and persist in his published writings and articles which are "contrary to our holy, Christian faith, which we and our forefathers have hitherto held, and to insist on it."[50] The condemnation of Luther is thus presupposed. Relief is only promised in the case of revocation. Thus, it is not clear what the purpose of this invitation to "hear" Luther should have been. Luther had the possibility to recant in Wittenberg, too. Or was this just a tactic to persuade the emperor to invite Luther, which was then expected to have its own dynamic? After the Imperial Diet in Nuremberg in 1524, Luther pointed out in his aforementioned publication of the Worms edict and the Nuremberg Mandate that the Imperial Diet had made two contradictory decisions: First, "I am to be treated in accordance with the outlawry that was imposed on me in Worms, and this commandment is to be carried out strictly, and in addition to this, the opposite commandment is to be accepted, that one

48. Ulrich Köpf, "Die Ausübung kirchlicher Lehrgewalt im 13. und frühen 14. Jahrhundert," in *Gewalt und ihre Legitimation im Mittelalter,* ed. Günther Mensching (Würzburg: Königshausen & Neumann, 2003), 155.

49. *Die Depeschen des Nuntius Aleander vom Wormser Reichstage 1521,* trans. and commented on by Paul Kalkoff (Halle: Verein für Reformationsgeschichte, 1886), 43.

50. RTA 2:516.14–15.

should first of all negotiate at the future Diet what is good and bad about my teaching. There I am condemned *and* spared for the coming trial."[51] This shows that on the one hand the estates were clinging to the traditional ecclesiastical jurisdiction and its realization by the temporal authorities, and yet some of them also realized that all this had become fragile, because the old procedures were not appropriate for addressing what was new in Luther's theology. This widespread impression of impropriety took away the inner strength of the conventional procedures in dealing with heresy. The Edict of Worms itself conceals this; the failure to implement it everywhere in the German Reich shows it clearly.

In a sharp comment on the mandate of the Nuremberg Reichstag in 1524, which was issued in the name of the emperor, Luther wrote:

> Here you see how the poor, mortal sack of maggots, the emperor, who is not for a moment sure of his life, brazenly boasts that he is the true, supreme protector of the Christian faith. The Holy Scripture says that the Christian faith is a rock stronger than the devil, death and all power (Matthew 16:18) and a divine power (Rom 1:16). And such a power should be protected by a child of death, whom even a scab or pock can tie to bed?[52]

Had Luther with these strong words also considered how much he owed the preservation of his very life to the protecting hand of his electoral prince? In these words, Luther may have underestimated the role of the princes and magistrates in promoting and protecting the Reformation movement in some areas or in its suppression in others, as in Austria or Slovenia. With regard to the Edict of Worms, it is particularly evident that Frederick the Wise, through clever politics and diplomacy, managed to prevent the edict from being put into effect in electoral Saxony.

When it comes to the edict, we always have to consider Emperor Charles V. Luther's words just quoted bring to mind what biographer Heinz Schilling wrote about the emperor's life record:

> Tragic is the contrast between pretended majesty and his performance as a ruler. In the end, the Emperor had missed the goals that he had pursued throughout his life as a mission received from God. Instead of the new peaceful order for the Holy Roman Empire and Europe, Germany was torn apart internally, and the European powers were facing each other more hostilely than ever before. Instead of the longed-for unity and integrity of the church, Christendom had fallen into the fundamental enmity of

51. WA 15:254.15–19 (emphasis added).
52. WA 15:278.1–7.

the denominations. The Church, for him and his house the one, holy, Catholic and Apostolic Church had become a particular church [. . .] The first emperor of a world empire had to capitulate to the centrifugal forces of the new age and admit to himself that his world had been shattered. Wherever he wanted to create harmony, law, and order, he became a party, in the struggle for the political order of Europe as well as in the struggle for reform of the church. [. . .] In only five years, the wheel of Fortune had torn him down from the height of the victorious emperor, who in 1547/48 dictated his terms to the defeated at the 'harnessed Reichstag' of Augsburg, into the misery of a refugee.[53]

Luther's words seem to have a prophetic dimension. The emperor did not preserve the unity of the empire and was unable to achieve the reform of the church as he thought it should be. This also applies to the Edict of Worms. But even the pure word of the gospel, which Luther was convinced had been brought back to light by the reformers, did not lead to the reform of the whole church. Thus, the Edict of Worms has become a document of the division of Christianity and Europe.

FOR FURTHER READING

Brecht, Martin. *Martin Luther: His Road to the Reformation, 1483–1521.* Translated by James L. Schaaf. Minneapolis: Fortress, 1985.

Kohnle, Armin. *Reichstag und Reformation: Kaiserliche und ständische Religionspolitik von den Anfängen der Causa Lutheri bis zum Nürnberger Religionsfrieden.* Gütersloh: Gütersloher, 2001.

Parker, Geoffrey. *Emperor: A New Life of Charles V.* New Haven: Yale University Press, 2019.

53. Schilling, *Karl V.*, 10–12.

Original Publications of Respective Quincenntennials

Wengert, Timothy J. "The *95 Theses* as Luther's Template for Reading Scripture." *Lutheran Quarterly* 31/3 (2017): 249–66.

Hopman, Nicholas. "The Heidelberg Disputation; April 26, 1518." *Lutheran Quarterly* 31/4 (2017): 436–44.

Hequet, Suzanne. "The 1518 Proceedings at Augsburg." *Lutheran Quarterly* 32/1 (2018) 60–70.

Hendel, Kurt K. "The 1519 Leipzig Debate." *Lutheran Quarterly* 32/4 (2018): 446–54.

Hendel, Kurt K. "To the Christian Nobility of the German Nation—1520." *Lutheran Quarterly* 33/2 (2019): 188–96.

Johnson, Anna Marie. "Luther's 1520 *Treatise on Good Works*. *Lutheran Quarterly* 33/4 (2019): 373–85.

Herrmann, Erik. "The *Babylonian Captivity* (1520)." *Lutheran Quarterly* 34/1 (2020): 71–81.

Tranvik, Mark D. "The Freedom of a Christian (1520)." *Lutheran Quarterly* 34/1 (2020): 82–92.

Serina, Richard J. "The Excommunication of Martin Luther: *Exsurge Domine* (1520) and *Decet Romanum Pontificem* (1521)." *Lutheran Quarterly* 34/2 (2020): 194–208.

Dieter, Theodor. "*The Edict of Worms* (1521)." *Lutheran Quarterly* 35/1 (2021): 1–17.